KU-428-561

# BOOST YOUR
# ENERGY LEVELS
## NATURALLY

# BOOST YOUR
# ENERGY LEVELS
## NATURALLY

OVER 350 TECHNIQUES AND TIPS,
ILLUSTRATED WITH MORE THAN
800 PRACTICAL PHOTOGRAPHS

southwater

Southwater is an imprint of
Anness Publishing Ltd
Hermes House, 88–89
Blackfriars Road, London SE1
8HA; tel. 020 7401 2077;
fax 020 7633 9499
info@anness.com

© Anness Publishing Ltd
2006

UK agent: The Manning
Partnership Ltd, 6 The Old
Dairy, Melcombe Road, Bath
BA2 3LR; tel. 01225 478444;
fax 01225 478440;
sales@manning-
partnership.co.uk

UK distributor: Grantham
Book Services Ltd,
Isaac Newton Way, Alma Park
Industrial Estate, Grantham,
Lincs NG31 9SD;
tel. 01476 541080;
fax 01476 541061;
orders@gbs.tbs-ltd.co.uk

North American
agent/distributor: National
Book Network, 4501 Forbes
Boulevard, Suite 200,
Lanham, MD 20706;
tel. 301 459 3366;
fax 301 429 5746;
www.nbnbooks.com

Australian agent/distributor:
Pan Macmillan Australia,
Level 18, St Martins Tower, 31
Market St, Sydney,
NSW 2000; tel. 1300 135 113;
fax 1300 135 103;
customer.service@macmillan.
com.au

New Zealand
agent/distributor:
David Bateman Ltd, 30
Tarndale Grove, Off Bush
Road, Albany, Auckland;
tel. (09) 415 7664;
fax (09) 415 8892

All rights reserved. No part of this publication may be
reproduced, stored in a retrieval system, or transmitted in
any way or by any means, electronic, mechanical,
photocopying, recording or otherwise, without the prior
written permission of the copyright holder.

A CIP catalogue record for this book is available from the
British Library.

**Publisher**: Joanna Lorenz
**Editorial Director**: Helen Sudell
**Project Editors**: Caroline Davison, Melanie Halton, Simona
Hill, Debra Mayhew and Catherine Stuart
**Contributors**: Raje Airey, Jane Coney, Carmen Fernandez,
Gill Hale, Doriel Hall, Tracey Kelly, Simon Lilly, Sally
Morningstar, Rosalind Oxenford, Matthew Seal, Lilian
Vernier-Bonds and Vivien Williamson
**Designers**: Ann Cannings, Jane Coney, Lilian Lindblom,
Nigel Partridge and Ian Sandom
**Production Controller**: Steve Lang

Previously published as part of a larger volume, *The
Handbook of Alternative Healing.*

10 9 8 7 6 5 4 3 2 1

**Note**

The authors and publishers have made every effort to
ensure that all instructions within this book are accurate
and safe, and cannot accept liability for any resulting
injury, damage or loss to persons or property, however it
may arise. If you do have any special needs or problems,
consult your doctor or a professional practitioner. This
book cannot replace medical consultation and should be
used in conjunction with professional advice.

# Contents

# Introduction

**Natural energy is all around us in many forms, and much of it can be accessed by learning a few easy techniques or by making some simple modifications to lifestyle. By working in harmony with our natural environment, we can seek out some quite extraordinarily effective cures for everyday ailments.**

HARNESSING NATURE'S POWER

Natural phenomena such as colour, light and sound hold a wealth of vitality for those who know how to channel their subtle vibrations. HEALING WITH ENERGIES illustrates the effect of biorhythms and cosmic influences on stamina, and how to enhance the body's energy using simple diagnostic and therapeutic techniques such as kinesiology, dowsing, homeopathy, feng shui, mantra and water therapy.

The properties of gemstones have long been known to promote health and harmony, and a chapter on the dynamics of HEALING WITH CRYSTALS explores practical ways

▲ BALANCING WORK AND LEISURE IS A GREAT WAY OF MAXIMIZING ENERGY.

to harness the power of these valuable stones. Did you know, for example, that placing quartz near to your computer helps to combat the effects of electro-magnetism, or that headaches can be soothed by contact with healing amethysts?

Both this and a subsequent chapter on using COLOUR to heal explain the links between the seven chakras – which materalize as seven layers of coloured light – and natural energy flow. By applying the principles of full-body chakra healing to your choice, and usage, of crystals and colour, you

▼ HEALING MASSAGE CAN BE PRACTISED ON FAMILY MEMBERS YOUNG AND OLD.

▲ LIGHT, COLOUR AND CERTAIN GEMSTONES ARE POWERFUL ENERGY SOURCES.

can balance, energize or soothe through adjustments to your home and work environment.

### THERAPEUTIC TOUCH

The HANDS have long been used as instruments of healing, and a number of hands-on therapies have evolved to combat pain, boost immunity and increase stamina. Shiatsu is a holistic method of healing whereby finger pressure is applied to key points on the body to bring the female yin and male yang energies into balance. Reiki healing – which has roots in Tibetan Buddhism – works by harnessing the invisible energies of the cosmos and directing them towards the body as a force for well-being. Like shiatsu, reflexology works with finger pressure, by stimulating the body's energies through contact with the hands and feet.

### MIND OVER MATTER

Health practitioners are learning that many physical problems begin with prolonged and negative stress on the mind, which, if left unchecked, can weaken the body and open it to nasty ailments. It is vitally important to regain control of our emotional being. To this end, a chapter on HEALING WITH YOGA AND MEDITATION seeks to unite body and mind through a

▲ EATING THE RIGHT KINDS OF FOOD DOES WONDERS FOR EVERDAY ENERGY LEVELS.

series of easily-learned yet dynamic postures, techniques for better breathing and simple visualizations to promote focus, fitness, balance and resolve. The recommended meditations draw inspiration from the immediate environment and personal achievements to enable the individual to regain clarity, assess priorities and take positive action for the future.

# HEALING WITH
# ENERGIES

The link between the Earth's natural energy and the human condition has been recognized by cultures across the world since time began. Indeed, humankind has striven to tap into this invisible life force, learning to harness the subtle vibrations of colour, light and sound, the energies of plants and minerals, and the cosmic power of the sun and moon.

This section explains how to diagnose and treat energy imbalances using both ancient and modern methods, from acupuncture and feng shui to Vega testing and radionics. It also describes how energy therapies can help with common health problems, including chronic fatigue, allergies and emotional stress, and with physical discomfort such as arthritis.

# What is energy?

**Energy is life. It is the invisible force that animates the human body and permeates everything in the natural world, including animals, plants, trees and rocks, as well as the earth, sun, moon and stars.**

THE LIFE FORCE

Throughout the course of history, cultures all over the world have acknowledged the existence of a universal energy force flowing through everything in the world, including the human body. It has been given many names. In India it is referred to as "prana", in the Far East it is "chi" or "ki", while in some shamanist traditions it is described as "chula" or "animu". Today, many people refer to it as "spirit" or the "life force".

Invisible like the air we breathe, the life force has a powerful influence on our health and well-being. It not only governs our physical health and survival, but also our mental and emotional well-being; it is the spark that fuels our ambitions, driving us to express our personal creativity and strive to fulfil our spiritual potential.

Good health is achieved when the life force is balanced and allowed to flow freely. When it is blocked or unbalanced, it leads to disturbances that will eventually manifest as "dis-ease" or a state of disharmony in the natural order. Energy healing is all about finding ways to strengthen, balance and free up this energy by using naturally occurring vibrations, such as light or colour, or the energies of natural forms such as plants and crystals.

▾ A MASSIVE TREE STARTS LIFE AS A SEED THAT IS PULSING WITH LIFE FORCE ENERGY AS WELL AS THE POTENTIAL FOR GROWTH.

▲ WHEN THE LIFE FORCE IS IN HARMONY YOU FEEL READY TO TAKE ON THE WORLD.

▲ BY TAKING CARE OF OURSELVES, WE GIVE THE BODY A CHANCE TO REPLENISH LOST ENERGY.

## A UNIVERSE OF ENERGY

The life force connects us to the world we live in, weaving the fabric of life seamlessly together. Everything within the universe vibrates with energy and the world that we are part of is a vast web of energy patterns.

This idea has been verified by modern science. All matter, however dense it may appear, is made up of energy: it consists of atoms, protons, neutrons, electrons, waves and particles, all vibrating together at different frequencies. We live in the electromagnetic energy field of the earth, surrounded by wave forms, from low frequency radio waves at one end of the spectrum to high frequency cosmic rays at the other. Everything in the universe is made up of energy, which becomes more dense (and vibrates at a lower frequency) as it forms into matter. We are energetic phenomena and our world is dynamic. Like everything else in our lives, our health is influenced by the invisible energies that flow through us and swirl all around us.

# Cosmic influences

**We are part of the cosmic web of life delicately connected and held in balance by subtle energy forces. Changes in any part of this energy system will have a "knock-on" effect on our health and vitality – for better or worse.**

### THE SUN

At the centre of our solar system, the sun is a fireball of light and heat, and is our most important energy source. It creates the conditions for life on earth and influences our health and vitality. When someone is sick, it is as though their "light" has dimmed. The word "influenza" comes from an Italian word meaning "to influence", and research indicates that all the major flu epidemics of the last 250 years (including the 1918 flu pandemic) have coincided with increased solar activity.

### THE MOON

Lunar power controls the tides, affects weather, and influences human moods and behaviour. A woman's 28-day menstrual cycle follows the phases of the moon. The moon is also associated with psychological disturbances: the full moon is known as the time of lunacy or "moon madness", and its powerful energy can trigger such problems as epileptic fits, as well as increasing the potential for accidents.

### BIORHYTHMS

The forces of the sun and the moon are often thought of as masculine and feminine energies respectively. The male solar energy is focused on action in the world outside, on ambition and achievement, while the female lunar energy is inwardly focused,

◀ BECAUSE THE SUN IS SO CRITICAL TO LIFE, IT WAS HELD IN AWE BY MANY EARLY CIVILIZATIONS AND REVERED AS A GOD. EVEN TODAY, PEOPLE DESCRIBE THEMSELVES AS "SUN-WORSHIPPERS".

◄ COLLECTING APPLES AT HARVEST TIME REMINDS US OF NATURE'S CYCLES AND THE CHANGING SEASONS OF THE YEAR.

world", while at other times we feel lethargic and find it more difficult to get things done.

### THE SEASONS

The changing seasons also affect our energy levels and many illnesses are seasonal. Light deprivation is thought to be associated with seasonal affective disorder (SAD), which is a severe manifestation of the "winter blues". We suffer more colds and flu in winter, whereas early summer is the hayfever season.

and more concerned with the intuitive world of feelings and emotion. According to the theory of biorhythms, we all have an internal male "solar" cycle and a female "lunar" cycle that affects us physically, emotionally and intellectually. These cycles produce a pattern of highs and lows, so that some days we may have lots of energy and feel "on top of the

▼ BOTH MEN AND WOMEN CONTAIN A BALANCE OF FEMININE AND MASCULINE ENERGIES, ALSO KNOWN AS YIN AND YANG.

# The human energy field

**There is more to the human form than meets the eye. The vital force emanates around the body like a luminous sphere or "aura", entering through the chakras and running along energy pathways, or meridians.**

THE AURA

The body's aura is subtle energy that vibrates at a different wavelength and frequency to the energy of the physical body. It is sometimes seen or depicted as a halo and may be felt when someone "enters your space". Auras vary in size, density and colour, but their overall size, shape and vibrancy is indicative of your state of health. The healthier you are, the larger and brighter your aura; when you are sick, your aura contracts as the body tries to conserve its vital energy. The size of the aura can also depend on mood and place.

SUBTLE ANATOMY

The energy pod around the human form can be visualized as seven layers of light, each vibrating at a higher frequency than the previous one. These layers are also known as the

## THE SUBTLE BODIES

**1** Etheric body: closest to the physical body; provides a blueprint for the physical body and its organs.
**2** Emotional body: the seat of the emotions.
**3** Mental body: mental activity, thoughts, ideas and day-to-day concerns.
**4** Astral body: represents the personality.
**5** Causal body: seat of willpower and gateway to higher consciousness; fulfilment of personal destiny.
**6** Celestial soul body: spiritual essence, sometimes referred to as the "higher self".
**7** Illuminated spiritual body: the highest and most refined level, where we become one with the source of love and healing, or the Divine.

▲ WE ARE MOST AWARE OF HUMAN ENERGY FIELDS WHEN WE SENSE THE MOOD OF SOMEONE CLOSE BY, OR FEEL OUR "SPACE" IS BEING INVADED WHEN ANOTHER PERSON COMES TOO NEAR TO US.

"subtle bodies", and each one has a particular function. The energy of these subtle bodies enters and leaves our system through the chakras, moving along energy channels known as "nadis" or "meridians".

Some people can discern auras around our physical body, and almost anyone can be taught to sense the different qualities within a person's auric field. Like the chakras, each level of the subtle bodies represents a certain frequency of personal energy.

The Indian philosophers and yogis of old described complex patterns in our "subtle bodies", and identified different energy systems beyond the physical:

• the etheric body is closest to the physical and provides the blueprint for the body and its organs. A disruption of harmony within the etheric almost always precedes physical illness;

• the emotional body contains our ever-changing patterns of emotions and feelings. As the least stable of the subtle bodies, it is therefore the easiest one to

modify with techniques such as crystal healing.

• the mental body contains the patterns in which we have organized our understanding of reality, with our beliefs and ideas, and everyday thinking;

• the finer subtle bodies are concerned with our spiritual identity and our connection with the universal or "collective unconscious". It is less easy to define these subtle areas of life, although, as you become more familiar with the practice of energy healing, you will learn to detect and balance them.

▶ THE SUBTLE BODIES ARE THE FINE, NON-PHYSICAL LEVELS OF OUR BEING.

# Energy and health

**Good health is achieved when our energy levels are in a state of balance. When they are depleted or out of balance, we become sick and unhappy. Living in balance and coping with change is the key to health.**

ENERGY BALANCING

Chronic illnesses are on the increase, yet we tend to take our health for granted, paying attention only when something goes wrong. As we strive to meet the pressures of modern living, we push beyond our limits and "run on empty". We need to achieve a balance between the quality and quantity of the energy we give out and what we take in. This means balancing work and leisure, rest and exercise, by ensuring we have enough sleep and eating a balanced diet. If we take in too much of the "wrong" sort of energy, our systems become clogged up or blocked. This creates imbalance, first in the "subtle bodies" (layers of energy around the body), and eventually in the physical body.

THE EFFECTS OF STRESS

Many illnesses are stress-related, including digestive disorders such as irritable bowel syndrome (IBS), respiratory conditions such as asthma, high blood pressure and painful tension headaches. Stress is one of the biggest causes of energy imbalance; it affects us in many ways and at many levels. Negative mental and emotional states, such as anxiety, grief, fear, anger, worry and also depression, create turbulence in the subtle energy bodies and will lead to physical complaints if the imbalances are not corrected.

◀ OVERWORK CAN LEAD TO MENTAL AND EMOTIONAL STRESS, WHICH AFFECTS RELATIONSHIPS AND CAUSES HEALTH PROBLEMS.

▲ WHEN YOU BITE INTO A FRESHLY PICKED ORGANIC APPLE, YOU CAN TELL THAT IT IS BURSTING WITH VITAL ENERGY.

▲ KEEP A PLANT ON YOUR DESK TO HELP PROTECT YOU FROM THE NEGATIVE ENERGIES CREATED BY ELECTRONIC OFFICE EQUIPMENT.

We are also affected by "geopathic stress", which is related to the electromagnetic energy fields of the earth. One natural cause of variations in the earth's energy field are underground water courses or "black streams". These have been thought to cause ill health for centuries. Indeed, recent research has associated them with chronic fatigue syndrome (ME), although the energy waves of modern electrical appliances, such as televisions, microwave ovens, computers and mobile phones, are also disturbing the earth's energy field, and may, in fact, be contributing to "modern" illnesses, such as ME, in ways that we don't yet understand.

### COPING WITH CHANGE

Any point of change, or transition, is a critical time in life. This can be anything from a change in your personal lifestyle (such as getting divorced or married, changing job, having children, or moving house) to the changing seasons of the year or climate changes when we go abroad.

At a time of transition we should try to take extra care of ourselves, as the immune system is under increased pressure while we are attempting to adjust to a new or difficult situation. If we pay insufficient attention to our energy levels and carry on as though we are invincible, we will eventually get sick.

# Taking care of yourself

**Your vital energy is your most precious commodity, and is worth looking after. For health and well-being, tune in to your energy field and learn to recognize the things that increase your energy levels and those that drain you.**

ENERGY DRAINERS AND BOOSTERS
Take a good look at your lifestyle and use this guide to help you avoid the energy drainers and cultivate the energy boosters.

**Key** *x* = energy drainers
✓ = energy boosters
● = tip

FOOD AND DRINK
At the most basic level, food and drink is the fuel our bodies need in order to function. The closer it is to its natural, unrefined state, the greater the energy boost.

*x* Refined, processed food, white flour, sugar, alcohol, caffeine,

"ready" meals, microwaved food.
✓ Raw food, unsweetened fresh fruit and vegetable juices, sprouted grains and seeds, freshly picked salad, fruit, vegetables.
● Drink 6 to 8 glasses of still mineral water a day. This will help to keep your system free of toxins.

RELATIONSHIPS
The people in our lives can be our greatest source of pleasure, yet they can also be a major cause of energy depletion. Some relationships are unavoidable, but with others you can be more selective.
*x* People who don't listen, have no time for you, "take" but don't give, tell you what to do/put you down/criticize you.
✓ People who make you laugh and feel good, share the balance of power, listen, are appreciative and supportive.
● Have a satisfying sex life.

◀ MAKE SURE YOUR DIET INCLUDES PLENTY OF ENERGY-BOOSTING FOODS, SUCH AS FRESH FRUIT AND VEGETABLES.

▲ CHANNELLING ENERGY INTO PHYSICAL
ACTIVITIES ACTS AS A PRESSURE VALVE.

## WORK

Since work is a major part of life,
it's very important to find a way
of working that suits you.

✗ Working long hours, not getting
paid enough, "putting up with it",
feeling forced to do it, lack of
recognition.

✓ Enjoying what you do, getting a
proper reward and recognition.

● Try to make your work fit around
you and your needs; don't be a
"wage slave".

## TIP

Chronic illnesses are on the
increase. Improve your
resistance to disease by
improving your energy levels.
This will also help you to deal
with any existing illness.

## LIFESTYLE

Aim for balance in your activities
and avoid going to extremes.

✗ Lack of sleep, exercise.

✓ Regular exercise and/or stress-
reducing techniques, such as
yoga, pilates, meditation, tai chi,
working out.

● Make time for yourself each day.

## ENVIRONMENT

Our surroundings have an instant
effect on our energy levels.

✗ Packed city streets, busy shops,
fluorescent lighting, clutter, lack
of natural light and greenery.

✓ Nature, especially green leafy
forests or windswept beaches,
décor that makes you feel good,
clear and tidy work spaces.

● Relax under a large leafy tree.

▼ TAKE REGULAR EXERCISE. GENTLE
STRETCHING HELPS TO RELEASE TENSION.

# Technology and energy

**Technological advances in the 20th century have made it possible to measure the electrical energy fields of the human body. Kirlian photography and Vega testing both monitor energy patterns, using them for diagnosis.**

KIRLIAN PHOTOGRAPHY

In 1939, Semyon Kirlian, a Russian electrician, discovered a way of producing an image of the electromagnetic energy field that surrounds the human body. To take a Kirlian photograph, the body's electromagnetic field (usually via the hands and/or feet) is brought into contact with a high-voltage, high-frequency electric charge. A photograph is taken of the resulting "interference pattern". This pattern can then be used to detect the strength or weakness of the body's electrical energy field and shows where it is out of balance. A healthy body is indicated by a regular, bright field around the hand or foot, whereas a thin, patchy field indicates energy blocks or disturbances.

The pattern is affected by physical and emotional states. For instance, if you are in shock or exhausted, the energy pattern may not register, whereas if you are anxious or irritable, the image may have an erratic outer edge, with sharp points, rather than a smooth, even contour. The menstrual cycle, medication, as well as chronic or life-threatening illnesses such as cancer, also affect the energy pattern. Taking exercise, having acupuncture or other "energy-based medicines", meditating or doing yoga have all been shown to increase the radiance of the Kirlian image.

◄ KIRLIAN PHOTOGRAPHY IS ABLE TO DEMONSTRATE THAT THE AURA INCREASES IN SIZE AND RADIANCE DURING MEDITATION.

## Vega testing

Research in Germany during the 1950s showed that acupuncture points on the body (where energy is concentrated and linked to specific organs) had electrical properties. Various electronic devices were then developed to measure and map these points, including the Vega machine, which was developed by Dr Helmut Schimmel in the 1970s.

Vega testing is used as a diagnostic technique, particularly to detect allergies or intolerances. During a Vega-testing consultation, an electronic probe or stylus is placed on certain points, usually on the feet and/or hands, while you hold an electrode in order to complete the circuit. The machine

▲ Allergies, or over-sensitivity to certain foods, such as dairy products, are becoming increasingly common.

measures fluctuations in your energy field as the stylus is placed at different points, indicating which organs may be out of balance. Homeopathic dilutions of allergens, such as pollen, house dust, dairy produce, feathers or fur, can also be brought into the electronic circuit. An erratic reading is produced when your body is intolerant of a particular substance. The technique can also be used in order to verify which homeopathic remedies your body needs.

◄ It is possible to desensitize the body using homeopathic remedies of common allergens, such as dust or pollen.

# Diagnosis by dowsing

**Dowsing is an ancient art that can be used to diagnose energy imbalances and to detect invisible energy pathways. With a little practice, anyone can dowse. All you need is a simple pendulum and an open mind.**

### PRINCIPLES OF DOWSING

Dowsing is a method of divining or "tapping into" the intelligence of the life force to gain access to information. Holding a pendulum, the dowser will ask a clear, unambiguous "yes/no" question. The pendulum picks up on the energetic vibrations pertaining to the question and then moves in response. The direction of this movement indicates whether the response is positive or negative.

▼ A PENDULUM IS A POPULAR DOWSING TOOL. IT CAN BE MADE FROM METAL, WOOD, POLISHED STONE OR CRYSTAL, BUT IT'S UP TO YOU TO CHOOSE ONE THAT FEELS RIGHT.

### USING DOWSING

Dowsing is extremely useful as a diagnostic technique when you are working with healing with energies. For instance, you can dowse to check whether certain foods and vitamins are suitable for you, to detect allergies, to find out which colours, crystals or flower essences are helpful and even to find out where is the best place to live.

You can also dowse when giving healing, to find out where energy is blocked and to check when the energy is flowing again. The key to successful dowsing is asking the right question and remaining objective about the answer that comes back – it's rather like watching for the results of an internet search. Frame your questions clearly and hold the pendulum over the place or article in question. Reassess your findings at regular intervals to stay up-to-date with your changing needs.

## Tuning in

Before you dowse you need to establish the particular pendulum motions that will mean "yes" and "no" for you. Once you are confident and also familiar with the responses, you are ready to start dowsing.

**1** Sit upright and hold the pendulum over your lap. Allow it to swing back and forth. This is the "neutral" position.

**2** Move the pendulum over your dominant-side knee. State clearly in your mind, "Please show me my 'yes' response." Pay close attention to what the pendulum does as this will be your signal for "yes".

**3** Return the pendulum to "neutral", then repeat step 2, moving to your non-dominant side to find the "no" response.

## Pendulum responses

The diagrams show classic pendulum dowsing responses. Dowsing responses are a very individual and personal thing, however, and you need not worry if yours are not the same as these. What is important is that you are clear which response means "yes", which means "no" and which is "neutral", and then you work with those.

ANTI-CLOCKWISE FOR "NO"
TOWARDS AND AWAY FOR "NEUTRAL"
CLOCKWISE FOR "YES"

# Kinesiology

**Applied kinesiology, or muscle testing, is a way of finding and correcting energy imbalances before they become serious health problems. It can also be used to find the underlying causes of long-standing illnesses.**

MUSCLE TESTING

In the 1960s, George Goodheart, an American chiropractor, realized that muscles can tell us a great deal about our state of health. He found that the muscles could be strengthened by pressing, and by massaging other, seemingly unrelated, areas of the body. This is because the body is an integral whole, with all its major organs and systems connected by "energy circuits" or meridians. They power the system and link the muscles to different organs.

Excess or blocked energy in these channels can lead to weakness in the corresponding organ and can be detected in the relevant muscle. For example, the quadriceps in the thigh is linked to the small intestine; if you were sensitive to dairy products and drank a glass of milk, then the intolerance would register in the intestine, then in the quadriceps. By testing the strength of various muscles, a kinesiologist can work "backwards" to find out where the underlying problem resides.

▼ KINESIOLOGISTS ALSO USE MASSAGE TECHNIQUES TO BALANCE THE BODY AND TO STRENGTHEN AREAS OF WEAKNESS.

▼ DURING A CONSULTATION YOU WILL BE ASKED ABOUT YOUR MEDICAL HISTORY AND CURRENT MENTAL AND EMOTIONAL STATE.

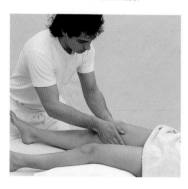

## THE TRIANGLE OF HEALTH

Kinesiology recognizes that there are three aspects to health – structural (or physical), mental and chemical – and that well-being relates to all three areas. A kinesiology session involves physical, chemical and/or mental "challenges" during which the patient is asked to resist pressure against an exerted limb. The muscle's energy circuit will "turn off" when an imbalance disrupts a particular pathway.

• Physical challenge: if your health problem is structural, pressure will be applied directly to the bones and muscles to find out where the problem is located.

• Chemical challenge: chemical substances, foods or homeopathic dilutions are placed directly on the tongue or skin, often in a glass phial. These tests are used for allergies.

• Mental challenge: you may be asked to focus on certain thoughts or feelings while the practitioner tests your muscle strength. In fact, many chronic illnesses have a strong emotional component, and you may find out more about the underlying cause of the complaint.

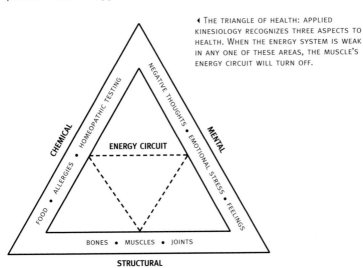

◀ THE TRIANGLE OF HEALTH: APPLIED KINESIOLOGY RECOGNIZES THREE ASPECTS TO HEALTH. WHEN THE ENERGY SYSTEM IS WEAK IN ANY ONE OF THESE AREAS, THE MUSCLE'S ENERGY CIRCUIT WILL TURN OFF.

CHEMICAL

NEGATIVE THOUGHTS

HOMEOPATHIC TESTING

ENERGY CIRCUIT

MENTAL

EMOTIONAL STRESS

FOOD • ALLERGIES

FEELINGS

BONES • MUSCLES • JOINTS

STRUCTURAL

# Acupuncture

**Acupuncture has been practised in China for thousands of years and is one of the oldest systems of healing. It involves inserting fine needles into specific points on the body to regulate the flow of energy through the meridians.**

### Yin and yang

In Chinese thought, the universe is characterized by opposing but complementary energies called "yin" and "yang". Together, they make up "chi" or the vital energy of the life force. Inner harmony is achieved when chi is balanced between these polarities and flows freely through the body, energizing and purifying the organs, tissues and blood. An excess or deficiency in either yin or yang, and/or blocks in the flow of chi, will lead to illness.

### Chi and the meridians

The chi is the energy equivalent of the immune system; it supports, nourishes and defends the whole person against disease. Chi runs through the body along energy channels or meridians, which are the equivalent of the arteries and veins of the physical body.

There are 12 main meridians – of which six are yin and six yang – and many minor ones. Together they form an intricate network. Each meridian is named after an organ or function. The yin organs, such as the liver, are "solid", whereas the yang organs, such as the stomach, are "hollow". Along

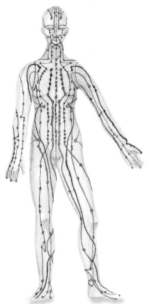

◄ FINE ENERGY CHANNELS, OR MERIDIANS, RUN THROUGH THE BODY, LINKING ITS SYSTEMS AND ORGANS. ACUPUNCTURE IS A TREATMENT THAT TAPS INTO THESE PATHWAYS AT SPECIFIC POINTS.

the meridians are approximately 365 acupuncture points where the chi is concentrated.

## TREATMENT

During an acupuncture treatment, extremely fine needles are gently inserted into the skin at the relevant points to stimulate or reduce the flow of chi through the meridian. This may produce a pulling or tugging sensation, but it does not hurt like a normal needle or damage the skin. Needles are usually inserted to a depth of 6–12 mm (¹/₄–¹/₂ in) and left in position for anything from a few seconds to an hour. It is usual for between 6 to 12 needles to be used, at a combination of acupuncture points. It is common to experience a heaviness in the limbs and/or feelings of deep relaxation. If the imbalance is due

▲ MOXA STICKS ARE OFTEN USED IN AN ACUPUNCTURE TREATMENT TO BALANCE EXCESS YIN (COLD AND DAMP) IN THE BODY.

to a yang deficiency, then the herb moxa (or mugwort) may be burned to generate heat. Dried moxa is rolled into a stick, which is lit and held over the acupuncture point until it becomes too hot.

Acupuncture is a very effective method of pain relief. It has been used in place of anaesthetics during surgery, in dentistry and in childbirth, and is widely used to treat back pain, arthritis and other chronic conditions. Having acupuncture usually leads to an increase in energy, an improved appetite and better sleep, as well as an improved sense of well-being. It should only be carried out by a qualified practitioner.

◄ MOXA IS USUALLY DRIED AND THEN ROLLED INTO CIGAR-LIKE STICKS.

# Reiki healing

**Reiki is a form of spiritual healing that originated in Japan. It works by drawing on "rei-ki" or universal-life energy, which is channelled to areas of need. Giving and receiving reiki is a gentle and relaxing experience.**

CHANNELLING THE POWER OF LOVE
The purpose of reiki is to work for the "highest good". It connects with the force of unconditional love, which transcends time and space and promotes positive living and compassion for all. To learn reiki it is usual to go through a special "attunement" with a qualified reiki master, using ancient and secret symbols to attune the physical and subtle bodies to spiritual energies and opening up a healing channel for them. This channel remains active for life, although the more you use it, the more effective it will be. You can visualize the force as a beam of white light, entering your body and flowing out of your hands when you give healing.

REIKI TREATMENTS
A non-invasive form of healing, reiki soothes away troubles and traumas in a peaceful way. Certain hand positions are used to dissolve energy blocks and re-balance the body. You can treat yourself with reiki, as well as others, and you can also use it to treat sick plants and animals and in the environment to guard against negative energy.

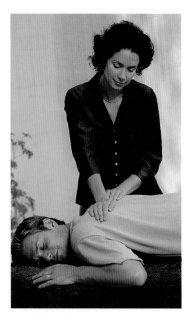

◀ THE PERSON CHANNELLING REIKI IS NEVER DRAINED, AS THE ENERGY FLOWS NOT FROM BUT THROUGH THE HEALER, RATHER LIKE WATER THROUGH A PIPE, AND INTO THE PERSON OR OBJECT BEING HEALED.

## Reiki refresher

A ten-minute reiki treatment will refresh and energize you and fill you with positive, loving energy.

**1** Place both hands over your eyes, close them and then relax. This helps to restore strained eyes and clear tension headaches. Move your hands to your temples to help clear an overactive or tired mind.

**2** Move your hands round to the back of the head and neck area, dispelling tension and refreshing the brain.

**3** Put your hands on either side of your neck. This helps the thyroid gland and the area associated with communication.

**4** Place your hands above the breasts in order to help with lymph drainage and the clearing of toxins. This position may generate some warmth.

**5** Finally, move your hands down to the sternum, fingers meeting at the heart chakra. This helps to restore emotional equilibrium. Finish with your hands below the navel to centre yourself.

# Homeopathy

**Homeopathy is a system that stimulates the body to heal itself. Homeopathic remedies are prepared from plant, mineral and other extracts, but diluted to such an extent that only the "energy" of the original substance remains.**

## LIKE CURES LIKE

Homeopathy has been an established system for about 200 years. Discovered by Samuel Hahnemann, a German doctor, it is based on the "law of similars" or the principle that like cures like: the symptoms caused by too much of a substance can also be cured with a small dose of it. For instance, in a patient suffering from insomnia, a homeopath may prescribe the remedy coffea (coffee), which in normal doses would cause sleeplessness in a healthy person.

▼ HOMEOPATHIC REMEDIES ARE PREPARED FROM NUMEROUS DIFFERENT PLANT, ANIMAL AND MINERAL SOURCES. THE ORIGINAL SUBSTANCE IS DILUTED MANY TIMES.

## REMEDY PICTURES

Homeopathy is concerned not only with physical symptoms, but also with your mental and emotional state, and remedies are selected on the basis of matching your overall "picture" with a suitable remedy. While two people may suffer from the same illness, they will not necessarily be prescribed the same remedy, as each person is unique. You can use homeopathy to treat yourself for minor acute illnesses, but for chronic conditions you should seek professional advice.

## ENERGY MEDICINE

Homeopathic remedies contain no chemical trace of the original substance. They are prepared through dilution and succussion (shaking) to leave only an energy "blueprint". This is then "broadcast" to your energy field, to stimulate the body's powers of healing on the mental, emotional and physical levels.

# Light therapy

**Light plays an important role in psychological and physical health, affecting our moods and immune system. Light therapy simulates natural daylight to treat a range of conditions, including skin problems and depression.**

## THE POWER OF LIGHT

Daylight is involved with the production of vitamin D, and sunlight also regulates the body's biological clock, affecting sleep patterns, appetite, temperature, sex drive and the production of hormones, including serotonin, the "happy hormone". Our biological clock is designed to be in tune with the natural rhythm of day and night, and seasonal change. Night work, long distance travel and extended periods of time indoors play havoc with our body chemistry, and light deprivation can lead to an impaired functioning of the immune system and depression.

## TREATMENT

Light therapy involves lying under a fluorescent full-spectrum, or bright, white light. This has the same effect as daylight, but does not contain the harmful UV rays. Daylight averages about 5,000 lux, whereas normal artificial light averages between 500–1,000. At least 2,500 lux are needed for a therapeutic effect. Professional supervision is recommended.

▼ SOAKING UP THE SUN IS GOOD IN SMALL DOSES. SUNLIGHT CAN LIFT DEPRESSION AND HELP WITH MANY SKIN PROBLEMS.

## TREATING DEPRESSION

Reduced daylight can cause severe depression. This is now officially recognized as a medical condition and referred to as SAD (seasonal affective disorder). It is often treated with light therapy.

# Colour vibrations

**Each band of energy in the colour spectrum vibrates at a frequency that corresponds with one of the body's organs and energy systems. Colour therapy uses light of the appropriate colour to restore equilibrium in the body.**

THE PSYCHOLOGY OF COLOUR

Instinctively we know that colours affect us in different ways. We speak of feeling blue, being in a black mood, being green with envy or red with anger. Every day and in countless ways we are influenced by the distinctive energy vibrations that each colour possesses, whether it is through the colour of our clothes, the food we eat, the rooms we live in or the scenery of the world outside. Colour is intrinsic to life.

▼ GREEN IS THE COLOUR OF FRESH GROWTH AND NATURAL HARMONY. IT SOOTHES SHOCK AND RELIEVES FATIGUE.

TUNING INTO COLOUR

It is not necessary to be able to see to have a sense of colour. Many blind people have, in fact, developed their sensitivity to the subtle vibrational energies of different colours in ways that we do not fully understand. For instance, the Aura-Soma colour system was developed in the 1980s by a British woman, Vicky Wall, after she lost her sight. The system uses colour essences in different combinations, which may be used in the bath or on the skin, to help balance emotional, spiritual and psychological states.

CHOOSING COLOURS

Use the colour vibration chart to help you select the colour that you feel is the most appropriate for you. If you are not sure which colour you need, use your intuition to choose the one that most attracts you. You can use dowsing with a pendulum to check your selection.

## Colour vibrations

Choose colours according to your healing need or preference

| colour | properties | healing uses |
|---|---|---|
| red | stimulating, energizing | low energy, sexual problems, blood disorders, lack of confidence |
| orange | cheering, enlivening | depression, mental disorders, asthma, rheumatism |
| yellow | inspiring, helping mental clarity and detachment | detoxifying, hormonal problems (menopause, menstrual difficulties) |
| green | fresh, vibrant, harmonious, idealistic | antiseptic, balancing, tonic, good for shock and fatigue, soothes headaches |
| blue | soothing, calming, promoting truth and inner reflection | insomnia, nervous disorders, throat problems, general healing |
| indigo | transforming, purifying | painkiller, sinus problems, migraine, eczema, inflammations, chest complaints, insomnia |
| violet/ purple | regal, dignifying | love of self, self-respect, psychological disorders and problems with the scalp (use sparingly, as purple is a "heavy" colour) |
| magenta | letting go | emotional hurts and upsets, accepting life's problems |
| black | absorbing, secretive | for when you need to hide (such as when grieving), or alternatively to convey an impression of power and control; self-discipline |
| white | reflecting, purity, innocence | a tonic; replaces all colours |
| gold | divine power, purity, the sun | depression and low energy, digestive disturbances, rheumatism, scars |
| silver | cosmic intelligence, the moon | hormonal and emotional balance, calms the nerves, for recovering equilibrium |

# Water therapies

Water is the elixir of life. It covers more than two-thirds of the earth's surface and our bodies are largely made from water. There are many ways of using water's cleansing and rejuvenating powers to increase health and vitality.

## DETOX TREATMENTS

Hydrotherapy is based on improving elimination of waste products, and there are simple treatments you can build into your daily routine. Drinking plenty of water will help your body flush out toxins and increase energy levels. Sweating expels impurities through the skin: vigorous exercise, saunas or steam baths are ideal. Take plenty of showers to wash away the toxins.

## HOT AND COLD

Cold water has a stimulating effect, constricting the blood vessels and inhibiting biochemical reactions that cause inflammation. It helps to energize and cleanse the organs and subtle energy system. Taking a cold shower seals the body's aura, stopping energy from leaking out.

Warm or hot water dilates the blood vessels, increasing the flow of blood to the skin and reducing

▼ GET INTO THE WATER HABIT. DRINKING BETWEEN 6 AND 8 GLASSES A DAY WILL HELP TO KEEP YOUR ENERGY LEVELS HIGH.

▼ RAW FRUIT AND VEGETABLES HAVE A HIGH WATER CONTENT. INCLUDE PLENTY IN YOUR DIET TO HELP YOUR BODY DETOX.

◄ WATER IS A POWERFUL CLEANSER. IT NOT ONLY CLEANS THE PHYSICAL BODY, BUT ALSO REMOVES PSYCHIC DIRT HELD IN THE AURA.

blood pressure. Warm water has a relaxing effect and can help to ease psychological and muscular tension by "drawing things" to the surface to be released.

### FLOTATION THERAPY

Combining the benefits of water with meditation, flotation therapy involves floating in warm water in an environment that is free from external stimuli. Salts and minerals are dissolved in the water to enable the body to float without any effort.

Sessions normally last from 1 to 1½ hours and take place in a sound- and light-proof tank or bath a little larger than the body. The water is maintained at skin temperature (34.2°C/93.5°F) and you can switch on a light or open the tank at any time. The effect is profoundly relaxing for both body and mind. The brain releases endorphins (the body's natural painkillers) and many people experience feelings of euphoria. Flotation therapy has a deep-cleansing and balancing effect on the subtle bodies and is particularly useful for treating stress and anxiety. It also helps to relieve hypertension (high blood pressure), tension headaches, back pain and muscle fatigue, and is a good immunity booster.

### HYDRATION

Some experts believe that dehydration underlies many health problems. Water helps to flush out toxins and keep the cells and organs healthy. Drinking 2–3 litres (3½–5½ pints) of water a day, cutting down on tea, coffee and alcohol – all of which are dehydrating – and eating more raw food (which has a high water content) is a good way to gain vitality. At first you may feel more tired, but after a few weeks you will notice that your energy levels increase and your skin will start to look fresher and clearer.

# Feng shui

**Dating back more than 1000 years, the Chinese art of feng shui is concerned with environmental influences on health and well-being. It offers practical suggestions of ways to balance the invisible energies in our surroundings.**

### Chi paths

According to ancient Chinese philosophy, our destiny is shaped by environmental forces, or the unseen energies that swirl all around us. Just as energy moves through the human body along the meridians, so it moves throughout the world around us, travelling along invisible energy pathways or "chi paths". Similarly, the energy in the environment is characterized in terms of the opposition between yin and yang. For instance, quiet and stillness are yin, noise and activity are yang. Round shapes, such as curves or circles, soft drapes and dark, absorbing colours enhance yin energy, whereas angular shapes and patterns, straight hangings and bright reflecting colours enhance yang energy.

### Balancing chi

The purpose of feng shui is to create an environment in which chi flows smoothly and an even balance between yin and yang is maintained. This helps to create the right conditions for growth – no matter whether you are trying to create a happy home life, a successful business or a beautiful garden. Chi that is out of balance creates stagnant or excess energy pools, which in turn creates disharmony and disruption, as well as possible sickness and exhaustion.

◀ For detecting chi paths, L-shaped metal rods are easier to work with than a pendulum. Keep high-use areas energetically clear and well balanced.

## WORKING WITH FENG SHUI

Landscapes, buildings, rooms and everything in them vibrate with energy. Human beings function best when they are in the same range of vibrations as the earth. Using natural materials in your home will help to promote positive chi. Synthetic materials, chemicals, microwave ovens and electrical equipment all create negative chi. To help balance the effects of this chi, use crystals and/or plants near computers and television sets, and limit the time you spend using them.

▲ KEEPING YOUR SURROUNDINGS CLEAN AND CLUTTER-FREE HELPS CHI TO FLOW SMOOTHLY AND PROMOTES A CALM ATMOSPHERE.

## DETECTING CHI PATHS

If you suffer from ill health or chronic tiredness, or your plans continually go awry, you may be exposed to negative chi paths. You can dowse to find the chi paths in your home and to indicate where chi is blocked or stagnant. Notice the health of any plants on the path and whether it runs under beds or chairs. It is best not to sleep or spend long periods directly in chi paths.

# Healing sounds

**Sound therapy is one of the oldest and most profound forms of energy healing. From the simple repetition of mystical words to complex rhythms and structures, sound waves can alter our mood and enhance well-being.**

A UNIVERSE OF SOUNDS

Sound is our first experience of life. In the womb, a baby becomes familiar with the mother's heartbeat and voice. We feel most at ease with naturally occurring sound frequencies, such as the human voice, a running stream, birdsong, or rustling leaves. Constant exposure to discordant noises and high levels of background noise, such as from traffic, undermines the sensitivity

▼ THE POWERFUL HEALING VIBRATIONS OF A GONG CAN HELP "CLEAR THE AIR" OF NEGATIVE ENERGIES.

## MANTRA

A mantra is a sacred sound that is used to "tune" the body's vibrational field and to raise levels of consciousness. In the Hindu tradition, the "om" mantra is believed to be the original sound from which the universe was born.

of our hearing and is a source of stress. Sound pollution weakens the immune system and has been linked to anxiety and depression.

VIBRATIONAL FIELDS

We pick up on sound waves not only through our ears, but also through our vibrational energy field. The subtle bodies, the chakras, and the physical body all vibrate at particular frequencies. When these vibrations are thrown out of balance, we are literally "out of tune", and become unwell. Sound therapy uses specific sound waves to retune these vibrations and restore harmony.

### USING THE VOICE

The voice is an almost unlimited source of healing energy. Simple ways to work with it include chanting, toning and singing. Tones are pure sounds held on a single note, such as "aaaaa..." or "uuuuu...". Practised regularly, toning has a powerful effect on the body's cells and can raise energy levels, help to release emotional trauma and promote mental clarity. It can be combined with chanting, which involves the repetition of a mantra or short phrase. Chanting is one of the oldest singing techniques and has its roots in spiritual traditions.

▲ MANY PEOPLE EXPERIENCE A SENSE OF EUPHORIA WHEN THEY HEAR THE HIGH FREQUENCY SOUNDS OF DOLPHINS.

▼ THE RHYTHMIC SOUND OF WAVES AS THEY CRASH ON THE SHORE CAN HAVE A CALMING EFFECT ON THE SPIRIT.

### MUSIC

Listening to music that is at the same frequency as alpha and theta brainwave patterns can promote relaxation and insight. Certain instruments, such as bells and gongs, generate particularly powerful healing sounds and their vibrations can be used to "clear the air" of negative energies.

### BENEFITS

Healing sounds can dissolve tension, regulate heart rate and breathing, increase mental clarity and raise consciousness. Some high frequency sounds encourage the release of endorphins, and can produce feelings of bliss and euphoria.

# Magnetotherapy

**Magnets have been widely used in healing for thousands of years. A magnet generates an electromagnetic field (EMF) that can be used to influence the body's natural energy circuits to treat many common complaints.**

## USING MAGNETS

Magnets have the ability to speed up the flow of liquids and to prevent the clogging of channels. This gives them many benefits. For instance, they can be fitted to water pipes to reduce the build-up of scale; the magnets create a magnetic field that keeps the positively charged calcium ions (the ones that cause the scale) in suspension and away from the inner walls of the pipe.

▼ PLACING MAGNETS AT STRATEGIC POINTS ON THE BODY CAN RELIEVE MENSTRUAL PAIN AND OTHER AILMENTS.

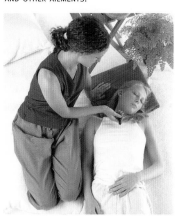

## MAGNET THERAPY

Magnets can improve the flow of blood through the veins. They can help to clear blocked arteries, improve oxygen supply to the cells, stimulate the metabolism, and help with the elimination of waste. There is growing evidence that they ease muscle and joint pain and reduce inflammation. Magnets can be used to treat a variety of conditions, including arthritis, respiratory disorders, menstrual problems, headaches and insomnia.

Magnetic healthcare products include straps and wristbands, mattresses, car seat covers and shoe insoles, as well as special devices to fit to plumbing and heating systems. The magnet is worn or placed either at the site of pain, over lymph nodes (to encourage the drainage of toxins), or at specific acupuncture points. Many wearers report increased energy levels, improved mental clarity and general well-being.

# Radionics

**Radionics is a method of distant healing that uses specially designed instruments to analyse and treat energy imbalances. It was pioneered in the 1920s by Dr Albert Abrams, an American neurologist.**

## THE WITNESS

During the course of his work, Abrams devised a special machine, which became known as "the black box", with which to read the pattern of his patients' energy fields. This pattern is held in every cell of the body and can be witnessed in any of its parts, such as a drop of blood, a nail clipping or a lock of hair. Provided any small part can be given to the radionics practitioner as a "witness", it is not necessary for the patient to be present during diagnosis and treatment.

## TREATMENT

You will be asked to complete a health-check questionnaire and send a hair or blood sample to the practitioner, to act as the witness, and to provide an "energetic link" between you. The witness is then placed on a black box and readings are taken to indicate your physical, mental and emotional state, your energy flow,

▲ A RADIONICS PRACTITIONER MAY ALSO USE DOWSING TO VERIFY HIS OR HER DIAGNOSIS AND TREATMENT PLAN.

any indications of major diseases and the cause of any existing health problem. Once a diagnosis has been made, the black box is used to "broadcast" healing energy to you. Some practitioners may also suggest homeopathic or Bach flower remedies, or colour therapy. Radionics aims to improve general health and well-being and is particularly helpful for diagnosing and treating allergies.

# ENERGY
# TREATMENTS

The therapies in this section aim to tap into the subtle energies of the universe, and attune them to the human energy field, to restore balance and harmony, and help you return to optimum physical, mental and emotional health.

The treatments range from healing medicines, as used in homeopathy or flower and gemstone essences, to harnessing and directing the healing powers of magnets, water, light, sound and colour. Many of these techniques can be safely practised at home with just a few simple accessories, but some, such as acupuncture and radionics, should only be carried out by a qualified practitioner. Always seek advice if unsure.

# Stress

**A certain amount of stress is healthy, providing challenge and stimulation, but when faced with too much pressure the body responds by working harder until finally we get sick. Many common health problems are stress-related.**

Financial pressures, problems in relationships, bereavement or divorce, moving house, getting married, noise and traffic are all common "stressors" that most of us cannot avoid.

Meditation, calming colours and healing sounds can all help to reduce stress levels. Kinesiology has specific techniques to help with the release of emotional stress, and will also check for any nutritional deficiencies. Ensuring that we are fully meeting our dietary needs is also an important part of the recovery process.

DOWSING FOR DIET
To check your nutritional needs, check your "yes" response to the question: "is the time right to dowse about my diet?" If "yes", use your pendulum to dowse in turn over the following key food groups: protein; fats and oils; carbohydrate; fibre; water; minerals; vitamins. You can then refine your quest to dowse over specific foods, checking to see if they are right for your body at this particular stressful time.

HOMEOPATHIC REMEDIES
These work to boost your "vital force" and are prescribed on an individual basis. However, some may be useful in acute situations:
• Ignatia 6c: soothes grief and disappointment
• Nux vomica 6c: helps with stress from overwork and irritability
• Sepia 6c: when you feel unable to cope, weepy and irritable.

◀ DOWSING FOR DIET WILL HELP YOU TO BOOST YOUR VITALITY IN TIMES OF STRESS.

# Depression

**Most people experience mood swings as well as the highs and lows of life. However, persistent worries, fears and tensions create energy blocks and we can get stuck on a "low" if we do not find a way to release the energy.**

There are many triggers to negative mood states, including worries related to your state of health, finances, children or relationship problems. Physical illness or hormonal changes, such as those of menstruation, childbirth and menopause, may also be involved.

To encourage a more optimistic mood, use cheerful and enlivening colours, such as yellow or orange, with a touch of pink if you are feeling emotionally upset.

Avoid wearing black, grey and dark colours, and over-exposing yourself to "negative vibes" in the environment: this can include reading too much distressing news. Plenty of exposure to natural light, especially sunshine, is very helpful.

▼ WHEN YOUR SPIRITS ARE LOW, FLOWER REMEDIES CAN HELP RESTORE WELL-BEING.

## BACH FLOWERS

There are several Bach flower remedies that can help with depression. Select the one that most closely matches how you feel.
- Gorse: hopelessness and despair due to a setback
- Sweet chestnut: utter dejection and bleak outlook
- Mustard: gloom descends like a black cloud for no obvious reason
- Willow: introspective, pessimistic; self-pitying
- Honeysuckle: dwelling on the past, lack of interest in the present

MUSTARD          HONEYSUCKLE

# Headaches and migraine

**Most "everyday" headaches are caused by stress and tension. They can range from a dull throbbing to an intense stabbing pain. Migraines are even more disabling, and are often accompanied by nausea and vomiting.**

Headaches can be triggered by a variety of factors, including toxic overload (from prescription drugs, caffeine, alcohol, or junk food), dehydration, low blood sugar, food intolerance, eyestrain, sinusitis, weather conditions and hormonal swings. Migraine triggers may include foodstuffs, such as red wine, chocolate or cheese, and attacks are exacerbated by stress.

Water is one of the best first-aid treatments for headaches and migraine, so drink a glass or two

◀ IF YOU FEEL A HEADACHE COMING ON, TRY DRINKING A GLASS OR TWO OF MINERAL WATER. YOU MAY FIND THAT THE HEADACHE JUST DISAPPEARS OR IS AT LEAST LESS PAINFUL.

at the first sign of pain. Splashing your face with water and lying down at the onset of a migraine is also helpful. Tension headaches may be relieved by a bath, sauna or steam bath. Alternating hot and cold will improve circulation.

The colour green is restful on the eyes and may help you to relax, while amethysts can ease tension headaches. For pain relief, press between the thumb and forefinger of each hand, or press your thumbs into the hollow areas at the base of the skull on either side of the spine, and tilt your head back for a few moments, breathing deeply.

◀ RELIEVE TENSION HEADACHES BY SPLASHING COOL WATER OVER YOUR FACE.

# Arthritis

**There are two types of arthritis. Osteoarthritis is the more common and is marked by degeneration in the cartilage that protects the joints; in rheumatoid arthritis the joints become inflamed and painfully swollen.**

According to the World Health Organization, acupuncture is an effective treatment for arthritis and it is increasingly recommended by conventional medicine. Regular acupuncture treatments can help to ease joint pain, stiffness and inflammation, and restore a greater range of movement to the joints.

Water treatments can also be effective; cold compresses can help to relieve pain and swelling, or alternate hot and cold will help to boost the circulation and ease stiffness. Check your diet using kinesiology, dowsing or Vega testing and make sure you are getting enough of the foods, vitamins and minerals that your body needs. Cut down on the energy-draining foods, particularly those that are acid-forming, such as dairy products, chocolate, wine, caffeine and sugar.

MAGNET THERAPY

Wearing a magnetic wristband is an increasingly popular self-help treatment for arthritis. It can improve the circulation and help to break down the toxic crystal deposits that have accumulated around the joints. The magnet should be worn on the inner wrist, next to the pulse point. Drinking plenty of water will help the body to flush out the toxins.

◀ ARTHRITIS CAN BE TREATED IN A NUMBER OF DIFFERENT WAYS TO ENSURE THAT YOUR LATER YEARS ARE ACTIVE AND LESS PAINFUL.

# Colds and flu

**Catching a cold or flu is a sign that your energy levels are depleted and your body's defences are weakened. Colds are often linked with seasonal changes in weather patterns, when the body needs extra support.**

In the early "sore throat" stages of a cold, drink hot lemon and honey and eat light meals. In the later stages, eating raw foods and drinking fresh fruit and vegetable juices will have a cleansing and energy-boosting effect, and can help with clearing mucus. Avoid tea, coffee, sugar and dairy products. Resting and giving your body a chance to recover is also essential; carrying on regardless will drain your energy further and, in the long run, may mean that it takes even longer to get better.

▼ RED ONION IS USED TO MAKE THE HOMEOPATHIC REMEDY ALLIUM CEPA. THIS IS INDICATED FOR COLDS WITH PROFUSE SNEEZING AND "CRYING" EYES.

COLOUR TREATMENTS

To ease a sore throat, wrap a blue or green scarf around your neck to bring healing energy to your throat chakra. Alternatively, drink blue or green colour infusions.

## HOMEOPATHY CURES

There are several homeopathic remedies for colds and flu.
- Allium cepa 6c: head colds characterized by sneezing
- Ferrum phos 6c: cold that comes on slowly, with a red swollen throat
- Nux vomica 6c: irritability, feeling chilly, watery eyes
- Kali bich 6c: blocked sinuses with yellow-green mucus
- Aconite 6c: sudden onset of flu, often at night, with chill and high fever
- Belladonna 6c: sudden onset of flu, with headache, fever
- Gelsemium 6c: "traditional" flu, with shivers, shakes, aching muscles, debility

FERRUM PHOS       KALI BICH

# Chronic fatigue syndrome

**Chronic fatigue is an extremely disabling condition for which there is no conventional medical treatment. It can be a symptom of a number of conditions, such as depression or anaemia, or may follow a viral infection, such as flu.**

CFS is a complicated condition. Its symptoms are a sign that your energy is severely depleted and out of balance. This means that you need to be particularly wary of "energy drainers" and cultivate things that give you energy.

Start by assessing your diet and lifestyle. Find out if you have any food intolerances or allergies; kinesiology, Vega testing, dowsing and radionics can all be used to check for this. Then, consider the impact that electromagnetic energy fields may be having on your health. Is your home or workplace an energy haven or is it draining you? Metal conducts electricity, so don't position a bed near a radiator, or sleep in a brass bed next to a power point. Protect yourself from the electric fields of domestic appliances and make sure your computer screen has low-level radiation. Work with feng

▲ TRY TO AVOID PROLONGED PERIODS WHEN YOU ARE EXPOSED TO STRESS AS THIS WILL DEPLETE YOUR ENERGY LEVELS.

shui to keep energy pathways clear, and use colours that enhance energy: purples and blues to boost the immune system, greens to lift depression, and yellows to promote a positive outlook.

▶ SPENDING TIME WITH FRIENDS NOURISHES THE MENTAL AND EMOTIONAL BODIES AND CAN HELP TO TRIGGER THE BODY'S SELF-HEALING MECHANISMS.

# Allergies and intolerances

**True allergies are very rare, but over-sensitivity to certain foods or environmental factors is relatively common. These over-sensitivities or intolerances seem to be implicated in many common chronic health problems.**

If you suspect that you may be suffering from an intolerance, the first step is to identify the key triggers that have a destabilizing effect on your immune system. Kinesiology, Vega testing and radionics will help you locate these. Use dowsing to check your response to common allergens. These include alcohol, caffeine, corn, dairy produce, soya, sugar, wheat, chocolate, tomatoes, moulds, pollen, house dust, animal hair, exhaust fumes, glues, paints, electro-magnetic radiation, fungicides and pesticides.

DESENSITIZATION STRATEGIES
The obvious strategy is to avoid contact with an allergen. This can mean making dietary changes and changing your washing detergent, for instance. Some allergens are unavoidable, however, in which case you need to reprogramme your immune system. Taking homeopathic dilutions of the offending substance, such as house dust or pollen, can help you to build up immunity. These remedies work rather like vaccinations, but on an energy level rather than a physical level.

▼ A USEFUL HOMEOPATHIC REMEDY FOR HAYFEVER IS EUPHRASIA (EYEBRIGHT), INDICATED WHEN EYES ARE RED AND SORE.

▼ IF YOU FIND YOU ARE INTOLERANT TO WHEAT PRODUCTS, IT WILL MEAN ELIMINATING CERTAIN TYPES OF BREAD FROM YOUR DIET.

# Digestive problems

**A healthy digestive system is crucial for health and well-being. Any digestive disorder, no matter how trivial it may seem, is a sign of an energy imbalance that needs to be taken seriously and treated accordingly.**

Many digestive problems are linked to poor eating habits, food intolerance and emotional stress. If you suffer from frequent digestive problems, test for food allergens and eliminate any triggers from your diet. Many people are intolerant of wheat, corn and dairy products without realizing it. Eat a diet that is rich in energy-building foods, and avoid irritants such as tea, coffee, strong spices and alcohol. If your digestion is weak, raw food and elaborate meals with rich sauces are best avoided; instead, follow a plain diet that includes lightly steamed vegetables, chicken, fish, tofu and wholegrain rice. Drink plenty of water.

▲ MANY DIGESTIVE PROBLEMS ARE LINKED TO EMOTIONAL UPSETS.

BACH FLOWERS

When the problem is stress-related, taking Bach flower remedies can help to balance the mental and emotional bodies.

- Walnut: helps with a change in circumstances, such as a new job, moving house or divorce
- Scleranthus: constant dilemmas, unable to make decisions
- Vervain: wired up, unable to relax, chasing perfection
- Impatiens: impatient and also irritable, always in a hurry
- Crab apple: when revolted by food as well as eating; cleansing and detoxifying

## TIP
A quick treatment for nausea and vomiting is to apply finger pressure to the acupuncture point that is situated about 3 cm (1¼ in) above the wrist on the inside arm.

# Skin problems

**The state of our health and well-being shows in the skin. Skin disorders can indicate problems with digestion or circulation or inadequate removal of toxins from the body. They may also be a visible sign of stress.**

If your skin problem is stress-related, you need to find ways to release tension. Aerobic exercise will boost your energy and encourage the body to unwind. It also helps the body to release toxins. Drinking plenty of water helps to flush the toxins out of your system; starting the day with a glass of warm water will also encourage a sluggish digestive system to work more efficiently.

▼ IF YOU HAVE PROBLEM SKIN, TRY STARTING THE DAY WITH A GLASS OF WARM WATER RATHER THAN A CUP OF TEA OR COFFEE.

▲ A MEDITATION BEFORE BREAKFAST CAN BE VERY CALMING AND SOOTHING.

The redness, dryness and itching of many skin problems indicates excess heat. A cold shower will help to redress the balance, bringing the energy back inside the body and closing the pores.

### COLOUR MEDITATION
A short meditation will set you up for the day; tune in and visualize which colours you need. Green, pale pink or blue are often helpful for aggravated skin conditions such as eczema or dermatitis.

# PMS and menstrual cramps

**Many women experience problems with menstruation. Fluctuating hormone levels, emotional stress and physical tension can unbalance the system, producing symptoms from extreme mood swings to severe physical pain.**

Magnets can help to ease period pain by improving the flow of blood to the area. Apply the magnet midway between the pubic bone and the navel and leave in position for up to ten minutes. This should help to relieve the cramp. Alternatively use a reiki hand treatment. Place one hand on the lower stomach and the other on the lower back; visualize healing reiki energy flowing through your hand, dissolving any tension and bringing peace and well-being.

## Moontime

The menstrual cycle mirrors the 28-day cycle of the moon. Your "moontime" is a time when your energy levels are low, and ideally you should spend more time relaxing so as to build your energy in preparation for the coming period. If you want to tune in to the cycles of the moon, moonstone is the ideal stone to work with. Moonstone helps to balance and relax emotional states. It can also have beneficial effects on all the body's fluid systems and ease tension in the abdominal area.

Apply moonstones to your body in a pattern that amplifies their potential for relaxing and healing. Place one stone at the top of your head, one on the front of each shoulder and one on each hip. Close your eyes and relax.

▼ To treat period pains, channel healing energy through your hands with a relaxing reiki treatment.

# HEALING WITH
# CRYSTALS

The stabilizing power of crystals has made them a natural instrument of holistic healing, thanks to their orderly atomic structure. By placing a crystal against an aching muscle, for example, healing energies are directed to the source of the complaint – often a tense and congested area – and the pain alleviated.

Crystals appear in many forms, each with its own healing properties, and can be used in conjunction with chakra healing to treat specific parts of the anatomy. Harnessing the potent and mysterious powers of these gemstones can be easily achieved at home, either with a particular layout for, or simple contact with, the body, through crystal essences or with a simple crystal lightbox.

# How a crystal is born

Our word "crystal" is derived from the ancient Greek term "krystallos", meaning "ice". The Greeks thought rock crystal was water that had frozen so completely that it could never melt again.

The Greeks were not entirely mistaken, of course, because ice is indeed the crystal form of water, and we call ice crystals snowflakes, and recognize their six-sided forms. Every substance, from water to carbon, or blood, will form crystalline structures given the correct circumstances of temperature and pressure.

▲ THE INTERNAL LATTICE STRUCTURE OF A CRYSTAL IS REVEALED IN ITS EXTERNAL GEOMETRY OF FLAT PLANES AND ANGLES.

Deep within the Earth's crust superheated gases and mineral-rich solutions find their way towards the surface along cracks and fissures at very high temperatures. As they cool, the atoms of the boiling gases and liquids begin to arrange themselves in regular patterns. These repeating three-dimensional patterns of atoms are known as crystal lattices. All crystals have their own characteristic microscopic lattice forms.

As the mineral solutions near the Earth's surface cool and the pressure drops, atoms from different minerals often combine to create more complex crystals. Usually harder minerals, such as diamond, emerald and quartz, form at a higher pressure and temperature, and have a dense lattice structure. Softer minerals, such as calcite and turquoise, crystallize at lower temperatures and have a more open lattice.

The structure of the Earth is continually changing, but the essential quality of all crystals is their very stable atomic structure. Whatever the outside force – whether heat, pressure, electricity or light – crystals always make minute adjustments to restore their internal stability and lattice form.

This unique orderliness and stability makes crystals valuable in modern technology. They are used in watches and lasers, and as switching and regulating devices in engines powering all manner of things from cars to space shuttles.

No one is really certain how crystals help in healing, but it may be that the very nature of crystals increases the levels of harmony in their immediate environment. Crystals are known to be the most orderly matter in the universe. Because coherence is a stronger natural force than chaos, introducing order into a disorganized state – for example, by placing a crystal on an aching muscle – can increase the chances of the imbalance or disharmony returning to stability and order.

Whether the imbalance in us is a physical illness or emotional or mental upset, our energy pattern has lost its order. The simple, powerful resonance of a crystal, with its locked-in power of ancient fire and unique purity of form, may help us reinstate our own balance and harmony.

▼ WHETHER NATURAL OR CARVED, THE INTERNAL ORDERLINESS OF A CRYSTAL'S ATOMS CAN INFLUENCE ITS SURROUNDINGS.

# Crystal variations

**Crystals come in all manner of colours, shapes and sizes. They consist of many different ingredients, determined by conditions, such as location, temperature and pressure. Here are some of their many types and forms.**

### GEODE

If a mineral solution crystallizes in a hollow rock cavity, and the rock then erodes, geode crystals are formed. Geodes can be of many shapes and colours, according to the type of original rock and minerals.

### PHANTOM CRYSTAL

These stones are so named because within the body of a phantom are smaller outlines of the crystal form. During formation, where a crystal stops growing and then begins again, a few particles of other minerals may settle on the faces, clearly showing the stages of growth. These are fascinating and beautiful crystals to look at and make good personal meditation crystals.

### FLUORITE CRYSTAL

This gemstone forms around a cubic lattice structure making interlocking cubes, octahedral and pyramid crystals. It comes in a wide variety of colours, though violet is one of the commonest.

### CELESTITE

This is soft stone, which is most often formed by the evaporation of water from mineral deposits, leaving a clear and delicate blue crystal.

### AMETRINE

As the name suggests, this is a mix of amethyst, giving the violet colour, and citrine, which adds the golden yellow. Both are varieties of the common mineral, quartz.

## ROCK CRYSTAL WANDS

Crystals can be microscopic in size or very large indeed, growing to several metres in length. Long, thin prisms of crystal can be effective healing tools.

## RUTILATED QUARTZ

A clear or smoky crystal, rutilated quartz contains fine threads of golden or orange rutile (titanium oxide) crystals.

## IRON PYRITES

This ore of iron and sulphur is a common mineral in the Earth's crust. It can form perfect single cubes, sparkly masses resembling gold and flat, disc-like clusters of crystal.

## AMETHYST

This is another form of quartz, whose purple or violet colour comes from iron particles in the crystal.

## CITRINE

A form of quartz that occurs when violet amethyst is subjected to heat, either naturally or artificially.

## BLUE LACE AGATE

From the chalcedony family of crystals blue lace agate is made up of tiny blue and white quartz crystals, in swirls or lines.

## AMBER

A fossil pine tree resin, amber is found in rich yellows, orange brown and deep reds and greens, often with trapped foliage or even insects embedded within.

## OPAL

Is a member of the quartz family with a high water content, creating the colourful play of light. It is microcrystalline with no regular geometry visible.

# The chakra system

Knowledge of the chakra system comes from ancient Indian texts. These describe energy centres or chakras in the body, with seven major points arranged along the spinal column. These chakras are used in crystal healing.

## THE SEVEN CHAKRAS

In Indian philosophy the chakras are the areas of energy near the spine where particular internal organs and systems are focused. Seven points are counted along the spinal column from the crown of the head down to the base of the spine. Each chakra is linked with a physical function and also a mental or emotional state; and each has come to be represented by a particular colour. By matching the appropriate crystals with the relevant chakra centres, it is possible to help restore natural functioning of the body at many different levels.

▼ CHAKRA IS AN ANCIENT INDIAN WORD FOR "WHEEL". WHEREVER DIFFERENT STREAMS OF ENERGY CONVERGE, A SPIRALLING DYNAMIC FUNCTION IS CREATED.

## CHAKRA FUNCTIONS

• the first or base chakra at the base of the spine is red in colour, and concerns physical survival, and energy distribution in the body;

• the second or sacral chakra, apart from its control of the reproductive system, is concerned with creativity and pleasure-seeking; its colour is orange;

• the third or solar plexus chakra, is located between the bottom of the ribcage and the navel. Yellow in colour, it connects with confidence, personal power and gut instinct;

• the fourth or heart chakra is at the centre of the chest, is green and deals with relationships and personal development;

• the fifth or throat chakra controls the power of speech and communication, including learning, and is a blue colour;

• the sixth, third eye or brow chakra is in the centre of the forehead, its colour is indigo and it supervises mental powers, memory and psychic abilities;

7TH THE CROWN CHAKRA STIMULATES PERCEPTION AND INTUITION AND MAINTAINS THE OVERALL BALANCE OF THE SYSTEM.

6TH THE BROW CHAKRA (THIRD EYE) IS CONCERNED WITH UNDERSTANDING AND MENTAL ORGANIZATION.

5TH THE THROAT CHAKRA GOVERNS COMMUNICATION, EXPRESSION AND THE FLOW OF INFORMATION.

4TH THE HEART CHAKRA GOVERNS RELATIONSHIPS, PERSONAL DEVELOPMENT, JUDGMENT AND COMPASSION.

3RD THE SOLAR PLEXUS CHAKRA IS CONCERNED WITH SELF-CONFIDENCE AS WELL AS PERSONAL POWER.

2ND THE SACRAL CHAKRA GOVERNS CREATIVITY, SEXUAL DRIVE AND PASSION.

1ST THE ROOT CHAKRA IS LINKED WITH PHYSICAL SURVIVAL, ENERGY DISTRIBUTION AND PRACTICALITY.

THE SEVEN CHAKRAS OR ENERGY CENTRES OF THE BODY ARE DEPICTED AS WHIRLING WHEELS OF COLOUR.

• the seventh or crown chakra is located at the top of the head, its colour is violet, and it oversees the balance of the chakra system and higher spiritual growth.

### THE SUBTLE BODIES

Health problems can arise when energy in the subtle bodies or chakras becomes congested or is under- or over-stimulated. The root chakra, for example, can become "muddied" by eating the wrong foods, and through lack of exercise. Or when it is not linked properly to the physical body, you are likely to experience low energy and persistent tiredness. Problems in one body or chakra can also have a knock-on effect on the others. Crystal healing aims to bring the subtle bodies and the chakras into alignment. During any healing process, health and balance is understood to return to the subtle bodies first. Once the vibrational pattern is restored, the physical body then returns to health at its own slightly slower pace.

# Crystal colours

The simplest methods of crystal healing combine the colour of stones with the appropriate chakra. The colour of a crystal will always indicate its main energy function, so it is useful to learn the basic properties of each colour.

### RED (BASE CHAKRA)

This colour stimulates, activates and energizes, but also grounds and focuses. Associated stones include garnet, jasper and ruby.

GARNET

### ORANGE (SACRAL CHAKRA)

A mix of red and yellow, orange combines their activating and organizing roles in boosting energy flows or treating blockages. Related minerals include dark citrine, orange calcite, carnelian, topaz and copper.

ORANGE CALCITE

### YELLOW (SOLAR PLEXUS)

The vibrant colour yellow is concerned with strengthening and preserving the body's systems (e.g. nervous, digestive and

AMBER

immune). The associated stones are amber, rutilated quartz, tiger's eye, citrine quartz and iron pyrites.

### GREEN (HEART CHAKRA)

As the mid-spectrum colour, green acts to balance our emotions and relationships, encouraging growth in all areas of life.

MALACHITE

Heart stones include bloodstone, green aventurine, malachite, amazonite, moss agate, peridot and emerald.

### BLUE (THROAT CHAKRA)

The blue chakra relates principally to communication, both within ourselves and from us to the outside world. Related stones are celestite, blue lace agate, turquoise and aquamarine.

AQUAMARINE

LAPIS LAZULI

### INDIGO
### (BROW CHAKRA)

Dark blue, or indigo, governs perception, understanding and intuition. Associated with this centre are lapis lazuli, sodalite, kyanite, azurite and sapphire.

### VIOLET (CROWN CHAKRA)

The traditional colour of spiritual illumination and service, violet also represents the mind's control of the body and the self. Related stones include amethyst, fluorite, sugilite and iolite.

AMETHYST

### WHITE

With qualities of universality and clarity, white is also connected to the crown chakra. White light contains and reflects all other colours, symbolizing the potential to cleanse or purify energy. Clear quartz, herkimer diamond, Iceland spa, moonstone and selenite are favoured white stones.

MOONSTONE

TOURMALINE

### BLACK

The colour black absorbs light as much as white reflects it. Black reveals the hidden potential of a person or condition. It holds its energies in reserve, grounds and anchors energy. Related stones include smoky quartz, obsidian, tourmaline and haematite.

### PINK

ROSE QUARTZ

A blend of both red and white, pink is associated with the base and heart chakras, and works to restore underlying balance. Pink stones include rose quartz, rhodonite and rhodocrosite.

### MULTICOLOURED

These are various, and their actions reflect their colour combinations. Rainbow inclusions can be found in many transparent crystals including quartz. Other stones are azurite-malachite, hawk's eye, opal, labradorite and ametrine.

AMETRINE

# Choosing and cleansing crystals

**All the crystals described in this book are relatively easy to find at a reasonable price. When building up a personal collection, aim for quality rather than quantity. Purchase stones that attract you and that you feel happy with.**

CHOOSING YOUR CRYSTALS

When selecting suitable crystals, remember that you will be placing stones on a relaxed, prone body, whether yours or somebody else's. So avoid stones that are too heavy or too small. Flatter stones stay in place better than round ones. Try to acquire at least two stones per spectrum colour.

Small natural crystals of clear quartz are often needed, so try to find about a dozen, each of around 2–3 cm ($^3/_4$–1$^1/_4$ in) in length. Small crystals of smoky quartz, amethyst and citrine have many uses.

A small, hand-sized crystal cluster of clear quartz or amethyst is useful for cleansing and charging your stones.

Larger single stones and tumbled stones are good to hold and as meditation aids.

▼ HANDLE YOUR CRYSTALS CAREFULLY, SINCE SOME ARE SOFT AND CAN SCRATCH, WHILE OTHERS ARE HARD AND BRITTLE.

## CLEANSING YOUR CRYSTALS

New stones should be cleansed before you begin using them. Cleansing removes unwanted energy from the crystals and restores them to their original clarity. Cleanse your crystals every time you use them for healing. Try the following methods:

• Sun and water: hold the stones under running water for a minute and place them in the sun to dry.

• Incense or smudge stick: hold the crystal within the smoke; herbs such as sandalwood, sage, cedar and frankincense are good purifiers.

• Sound: the vibrations of a bell, gong or tuning fork can energetically clean a crystal.

• Sea salt: put dry sea salt (avoid salt water as it can corrode crystals)

▲ MATERIALS FOR CLEANSING CRYSTALS INCLUDE SALT, WATER, A TUNING FORK, INCENSE AND SMUDGE STICKS.

in a small container and bury your crystal in the salt crystals for approximately 24 hours.

▼ CLEAN STONES ON A CRYSTAL CLUSTER (BELOW LEFT) OR SURROUND ONE STONE WITH CLEAR QUARTZ POINTS FOR 24 HOURS (BELOW).

# Techniques: know your stones

**When you acquire a new crystal, spend some time getting familiar with it and developing a sensitivity to its subtle energy field. Try these simple techniques, being aware of how you feel at each step.**

SENSING YOUR CRYSTALS

**1** Examine your crystal from all angles, then close your eyes and feel it as you hold it in your hands for a minute or two.

**2** Open your eyes and gaze at the crystal. Then close your eyes once more. Does the crystal feel the same as before?

**3** Hold the crystal in one hand, then the other. Also try holding it in both hands.

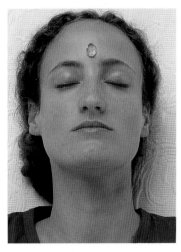

▲ LIE DOWN, CLOSE YOUR EYES AND RELAX AND SENSE THE EFFECT OF YOUR CHOSEN CRYSTAL ON A CHAKRA POINT.

**4** Now lie back and place the crystal on your chakra centres. The solar plexus, heart and brow are often good places to try.

**5** Still lying down, place the crystal close to your body, noting how it feels on the right and left sides, near your head and feet.

◄ DEVELOP A SENSITIVITY TO A NEW CRYSTAL BY HOLDING IT.

### A VISUALIZATION EXERCISE

This exercise is best done with a crystal you already know and feel comfortable with.

**1** Sit comfortably and hold the crystal in both hands. Relax and focus on it.

**2** Slowly let your awareness float down into the crystal and come to rest there.

**3** Think how the crystal feels – warm or damp, cool or dry, smooth or rough? Take a minute or two to explore its inner energy.

**4** Relax again, and attune yourself to the crystal's inner vibration or sound – is it a tone, a pulse or a tune, high or low, simple or complex? Listen for a few minutes, then relax again.

**5** Take some deep breaths, then imagine you are breathing in the crystal's energy. Does it have a taste or smell?

**6** Relax again, and open your inner eyes to imagine the lattice structure of the crystal, its inner light and landscape. Don't analyse anything you see, just let it come and go.

**7** Now become aware again of the crystal's taste, smell, sounds and touch. Gradually bring your awareness out of the crystal and back into your own body. Make notes so that you will be able to remember your experiences better.

▼ HOLD THE CRYSTAL NEAR YOUR SOLAR PLEXUS AND IMAGINE YOUR BREATH IS ENTERING YOUR BODY THROUGH THE STONE.

# Meditating with crystals

**Clear quartz can be a wonderful aid to meditation and contemplation. Just think, you are looking into solid matter of extraordinary stability and subtlety. Its constant harmony may help you increase or regain your own.**

If you are upset or stressed, gaze deeply into your favourite quartz crystal, and allow your mind to quieten down. When the body and mind begins to settle, it is easier to find solutions and balance.

Sit quietly with your quartz crystal and look closely at it. Then relax and shut your eyes. Pay attention to how you feel and think. Are your thoughts calm or busy, happy or sad? Note any sensations in your body.

After a few minutes, repeat the process using other quartz crystals and compare your experiences. Take deep, slow, breaths before you get up.

▲ SIT IN A COMFORTABLE POSITION TO MEDITATE WITH YOUR CRYSTALS.

Sit comfortably with a smoky quartz in your left hand and a clear quartz in your right. After a few moments swap them around. Do you feel any difference? Once you find a combination that suits you, try to spend a few minutes every day, preferably at the same time, sitting and meditating with your favourite crystals.

◀ GAZE INTO THE DEPTHS OF YOUR CRYSTAL AND CLOSE YOUR EYES.

### ACTIVE CONTEMPLATION

In another form of crystal meditation, place the crystal in a position in front of you that lets you gaze into its depths. Don't try to control your thoughts or worry about "doing it right". Just relax and enjoy the stone's company. Then close your eyes, feel calm, take some deep breaths and follow your thoughts. Open or close your eyes as you wish, but take the crystal's energy with you as you meditate.

If you find it difficult to relax and meditate with one crystal, you can make a pattern or mandala with your stones. This "active contemplation" may suit you better.

▼ MAKING A PATTERN OR A MANDALA OF YOUR STONES CAN CALM AN AGITATED MIND.

# Hand-held crystal healing

**We are all aware that positive thoughts are healing and negative thoughts are harmful. Using a quartz crystal in combination with directed positive thought can release a flow of healing energy, towards ourselves or to others.**

A quartz crystal will direct the energy either towards or away from your body, depending on where the point is facing. An additional crystal can be held in the "absorbing" or "receiving" hand. This helps us to feel the quartz's healing energy clearly in our awareness.

ENERGY CHANNELLING

If you have an area of over-excited energy, you may feel congested, hot, tense, irritated or frustrated. Place the palm of your left hand over that area. Hold the quartz crystal in your right hand, with its point away from you and towards the ground. Breathe deeply and evenly, imagining all the excess energy releasing from your body. Let it pass out through the crystal into the earth and away from you.

If you need to recharge depleted energy or want extra healing energy, the process is reversed. Hold the quartz in your right hand, pointing it towards the area concerned. Hold your left hand away from your body, with the palm facing upwards. Breathe deeply and evenly, imagining healing energies from the universe passing from your upturned hand, through the crystal and into you.

▶ TO RELEASE EXCESS ENERGY INTO THE EARTH HOLD A QUARTZ CRYSTAL IN YOUR RIGHT HAND POINTING AWAY FROM YOU AND TOWARDS THE GROUND.

 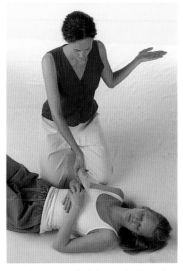

**1** To clear away unwanted energy, release tensions and help relaxation, hold your "receiving" hand close to your partner. With your "directing" hand, hold the quartz and allow the excess energy to drain away into the earth. Try moving the quartz in circles to aid the process.

**2** When you finish, revitalize the other person's aura by holding the crystal in the "directing" hand, with the point towards the body. Hold the "receiving" hand palm upwards and allow the universal energy to flow through the crystal into the newly cleansed area or chakra.

Try these exercises with opposite hands to see how it feels. Right-handed people often find their left hand more absorbing or "receiving", and the right hand directs the outward flow of energy. Left-handed people may find the opposite is true for them.

# Grounding and centring

**When you feel solidly anchored in the present, with a sense of inner calm and clarity, that is the experience of being grounded. Being ungrounded is a state of feeling confused and unfocused.**

GETTING GROUNDED

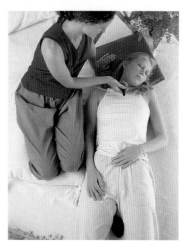

▲ ADOPT THIS LAYOUT TO CENTRE AND GROUND YOUR ENERGIES IN JUST A COUPLE OF MINUTES.

Holding a grounding stone can help us focus chaotic energy and restore everyday awareness. A simple grounding exercise is to sit or stand with your feet firmly on the floor, then imagine roots growing from your feet into the earth. With each breath, allow the roots to spread deeper and wider until you feel anchored and secure.

A GROUNDING LAYOUT

Lie down on your back and relax. Place one smoky quartz crystal point downwards at the base of the throat and another between the legs or close to the base of the spine. In most crystal healing patterns it helps to use a grounding stone close to the base chakra or between the feet and legs. Any changes created by the healing can then be more easily integrated into daily life.

▲ MANY OF THE CRYSTALS THAT HELP IN GROUNDING ARE DARK OR RED. TOP, LEFT TO RIGHT: SNOWFLAKE OBSIDIAN, HAEMATITE, DARK TOURMALINE, SMOKY QUARTZ, ONYX. BOTTOM, LEFT TO RIGHT: STAUROLITE, CITRINE, JASPER.

## Centring yourself

Feeling centred means being in a state of mental, emotional and physical balance. You know your boundaries and feel in control of your energies. Centring can be achieved by techniques that focus your attention within your body.

**1** Sit quietly, and be aware of your breathing. Feel yourself breathing in from your feet and back out through your feet into the earth.

**2** Be aware of your midline — an imaginary line extending from above the top of your head to below your feet, situated just in

▲ RESTORE YOUR FOCUS WITH A BLACK GROUNDING STONE.

front of your spine. Pull your breath into this midline from above and breathe out through the line into the ground. Repeat until you feel calm and focused.

**3** Strike a bell, gong or tuning fork, and listen for as long as the sound remains.

**4** Slowly and consciously bring your fingertips together and hold them for a minute or two. Take deep breaths in.

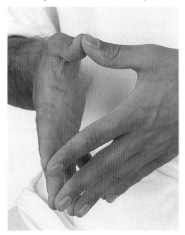

▲ BRING YOUR FINGERTIPS TOGETHER SLOWLY TO FOCUS YOUR ATTENTION.

# Pendulum healing

**Many people will be familiar with the idea of using a pendulum for dowsing. A pendulum made from a natural crystal can, however, be used as a healing tool in its own right, even if the individual has no experience with dowsing.**

Using a crystal pendulum for healing is effective in removing energy imbalances from the body's finer energy systems.

▲ THERE ARE MANY STYLES OF PENDULUM, SO CHOOSE ONE THAT FEELS RIGHT FOR YOU.

The healer has a clear intent that the pendulum will only move away from a neutral swing (back and forth) when it finds an energy imbalance that can be corrected quickly and safely. The crystal will move in a pattern that allows the imbalance to be cleared and will then return to the neutral swing. It is not necessary to know the nature of the imbalances – they may be on many levels from the physical, emotional, mental or spiritual bodies. Nor does the physical location of an imbalance necessarily indicate that it is where the source of a problem lies. The movement of a crystal's energy field through the aura simply helps to break up any build-up of unhelpful patterns, and releases them safely.

Whilst dowsing for assessment, any sort of pendulum, wood, metal, plastic, glass or stone can be used. Healing techniques using pendulums, however, will best employ a natural crystal. Because every crystal has its own range of properties the best crystal pendulums to use are ones that have a broad, generalized energy. These will respond to and balance many different types of energy imbalance. Clear quartz, amethyst and smoky quartz all make useful healing pendulums. Other clear and transparent crystals also work with broad ranges of energy.

As it is a healing tool, a crystal pendulum needs to be cleansed regularly before and after use.

REMOVING ENERGY IMBALANCES

▲ HOLD THE PENDULUM LIGHTLY AND FIRMLY
BETWEEN THE THUMB AND FOREFINGER.

1 Grip the pendulum. Allow the wrist to relax and hold your arm in a comfortable position.

2 Start the pendulum moving in a line, to and fro, in what is known as a neutral swing.

3 Slowly move up the centre of the body, beginning beneath the feet. Wherever the pendulum swings away from the neutral, simply stay at that point until the neutral swing returns.

4 When you reach the top of the head, go back to the feet and begin again. Now hold the pendulum nearer to one side of the body and again slowly move upwards. Repeat for the other side.

5 If the pendulum goes on moving over an imbalance for a long time, put another crystal on that spot and move on. Later check the area again. An appropriate choice of stone will have balanced the energies so that the pendulum remains in a neutral swing.

Although some methods place importance on the way a pendulum moves, in this technique any movement away from neutral simply indicates an imbalance that the crystal is able to correct.

▲ CRYSTAL PENDULUMS CAN HELP TO
BALANCE THE SUBTLE BODIES.

# Balancing the chakras

**One of the easiest ways to balance the chakra system is to place a stone of the appropriate colour on each area. This will give each chakra a boost of its own vibration without altering its energies or the system's overall harmony.**

SEVEN COLOUR CHAKRA LAYOUT
For this exercise use small stones, such as polished or tumbled crystals. Make sure that they have been energetically cleansed before beginning. If working on yourself, lay the stones near to where you will be lying so that they are easy to find and position. Even though you might sense little change, allow yourself a few moments to recover after having the stones in place for five or six minutes.

**1** It is a helpful start to place a grounding stone, such as smoky quartz, between your legs to act as an anchor.

**2** For the base chakra, place a red stone at the bottom of the spine or two stones of the same sort at the top of each leg.

**3** For the second or sacral chakra, position an orange-coloured stone on the lower abdomen.

▲ REST THE CROWN CHAKRA STONE AT THE TOP OF THE HEAD. CHOOSE CLEAR QUARTZ IF YOU HAVE USED AN AMETHYST FOR THE BROW.

**4** At the solar plexus use a yellow stone, positioned between the navel and ribcage. If there is tension here, put an energy-shifting stone, such as tiger's eye or clear quartz, on the diaphragm.

**5** Place a green stone in the centre of the chest to balance the heart chakra. Add a pink stone for emotional clearing.

**6** For the throat chakra use a light blue stone, placing it near the base of the throat, at the top of the breastbone.

**7** An indigo or dark blue stone positioned in the centre of the forehead is used to balance the brow or third eye chakra. Amethyst or another purple stone may also be tried.

**8** The crystal for the crown chakra should rest just above the top of your partner's head. If you choose an amethyst for the brow chakra, use a clear quartz crystal for the crown; if you used a dark blue stone for the brow, choose a violet crystal or gemstone to position at the crown chakra. It is always important to cleanse your stones at the end of a treatment.

INTUITIVE HEALING LAYOUTS

Once you become more confident in crystal healing or know the energies of the person you are treating better, allow yourself to be more intuitive in choosing suitable crystals for them.

**1** Lay your crystals on the table. Then, after grounding your energies for a minute or two, and with the person's needs in mind, pick up the stones that attract your attention. Don't think of colours or even of chakras.

**2** Place the stones where you feel they need to be on the body. Ask your partner how they feel, and make adjustments accordingly. After about five minutes remove the crystals and ground the energies with a smoky quartz.

▲ WHEN POSITIONING YOUR CHOSEN STONES TRY TO DO SO QUICKLY AND WITHOUT THINKING TOO HARD ABOUT IT.

# The crown chakra

**Located just above the top of the head, the crown chakra has a violet and purple colour or aura. It supervises and balances the chakra system as a whole and channels universal life energy into the system.**

Healing at this chakra will have an energizing effect on the whole body, though the effects may be slow to appear, because this most subtle of chakras works to clarify and harmonize the whole system. The crown chakra maintains our links to the rest of creation, feeding us much as the base chakra does.

Imbalances at the crown chakra can take the form of apathy and indifference, narrow-mindedness, loneliness

This is the centre at which imagination, inspiration, empathy and selfless service to others are nourished. Its colour is violet and purple, vestments of which are frequently chosen by secular and religious leaders to remind others of their power and authority. White, gold and magenta also relate to the crown chakra.

▶ TRY USING A CRYSTAL APPROPRIATE
FOR THE CROWN CHAKRA DURING TIMES OF
SELF-DOUBT, STRESS OR PROLONGED APATHY.

and lack of faith or belief. Sleep problems, stress and problems associated with learning may also be encountered.

CRYSTALS FOR THE CROWN CHAKRA

• AMETHYST is perhaps the most useful all-purpose stone used by crystal healers, and is especially popular as an aid to meditation. Amethyst acts to quieten the mind and will allow finer perceptions to manifest within us.

• FLUORITE exists in a variety of colours, often in the violet range, and it helps integrate subtle energies with normal consciousness, as well as aiding co-ordination, both physical and mental.

• SUGILITE can be useful in group situations, bringing greater collective harmony and coherence, and assisting those who dislike their circumstances and feel that they don't fit in.

• IOLITE is also known as water sapphire, but is no relation. It has a subtle violet translucence that stimulates the imagination and intuitive creativity.

• KUNZITE is pale pink and violet with a striated crystalline structure, and is good at removing emotional debris and helping in self-expression.

• CHAROITE AND ROCK CRYSTAL can also be used at the crown centre.

# The brow chakra

**The sixth chakra is located below the centre of the forehead, just above and between the brows, and is our "inner eye". Its colour is indigo and, like the crown chakra, it has been linked with the pineal and pituitary glands.**

This chakra is often referred to as the third eye, the single eye that looks deep within to see and understand as contrasted with the two physical eyes, which look outwards and receive optical data from the world of the senses.

The brow chakra is the "inner eye" of the imagination, creativity and dreaming. It "sees" hidden patterns and groups and grasps spiritual essences. This is a psychic place at the threshold of the inner and outer worlds, and is a natural seat of knowledge. It is no accident that when we think hard we often put our hand to this point to make our focus deeper.

Healing at this chakra can benefit many conditions linked to headaches and migraines, recurrent nightmares and bad sleep, depression and stress. The eyes, nose and ears can also gain much from treatments here, with eye strain, clogged sinuses and earache being eased with a

▶ To clear a blocked nose massage between the brows with lepidolite.

gentle application of an amethyst, purple fluorite or lapis lazuli. Poor concentration and memory can also be improved by using these stones regularly.

CRYSTALS FOR THE BROW CHAKRA
Indigo or midnight blue is the colour of the third eye chakra, and among the stones which have been found to work best are:

• LAPIS LAZULI is a rock of different minerals that can stimulate the rapid release of stresses and energize the mind.

• SAPPHIRE, which can relax and bring peace to the mind and balance all aspects of the self by releasing tension.

• SODALITE is similar to but less vivid a blue than lapis lazuli, and works to calm and open the mind to receiving new information and messages.

• KYANITE has a "fan-like" appearance and is favoured for moving on blocked energies and rapidly restoring the body's basic equilibrium.

• AZURITE also helps to unblock channels of communication and stimulate memory and recall.

• LEPIDOLITE and PURPLE FLUORITE are also often used to good effect at this centre.

# The throat chakra

**The throat chakra is concerned with the free flow of communication at all levels. It allows self-expression and personal creativity, enabling us to hear, learn and teach. Its colour and related crystals are light blue.**

On the physical level this chakra governs the proper functioning of the throat area, which under stress can mean conditions such as tight shoulders, tonsillitis, laryngitis or sore throats. Crystals can help lighten these blockages.

More generally this is the centre of self-expression, which often reflects our self-image. Any difficulty in communicating, whether caused by emotional or physical problems, can be eased by balancing the energies of the throat chakra. Attention given to this chakra may be of considerable value.

Unblocking the subtle energies at the throat centre will allow us to say our piece and be heard. Emotions can also become blocked here as desires rise from the heart chakra and are unable to be expressed because of external restrictions, such as social values and family expectations. Working at this chakra can allow creativity to flow again.

▶ THROAT COMPLAINTS CAN BE TREATED BY WORKING THIS CHAKRA.

When stressed, we can often feel pressure on our neck and shoulders. A light blue crystal placed near the throat can quickly alleviate symptoms. This centre can often feel restricted in a healing session as stress is released. An appropriate stone will help to ease the flow and promote a relaxed sense of peace and openness.

CRYSTALS FOR THE THROAT CHAKRA

• TURQUOISE has been valued since ancient times as a supportive and protective stone, which can strengthen the subtle bodies and the fine communication systems within the body.

• AQUAMARINE is a blue variety of beryl and a stimulator of the body's own healing systems; it also supports efforts to stand our ground and be honest with our feelings.

• BLUE LACE AGATE is a banded form of blue quartz that will calm and soothe, while at the same time lighten our thoughts.

• CELESTITE forms a delicate blue crystal that is "dreamy" in quality. It helps to lift heavy moods and to express spiritual needs. It is also useful for throat problems.

• SAPPHIRE and SODALITE, also used for the brow chakra, can be valuable alternative crystals to try out at the throat centre.

# The heart chakra

Located midway in the chakra system, the heart centre is associated with the colour green – the middle of the spectrum of light. The heart chakra is thus a place of balance, harmony and equilibrium at all levels.

have seriously life-damaging effects on the majority of animals, including humans. Restriction, even if it is only imaginary, depletes the immune system allowing disease and illness to take hold. Balancing the energies of the heart chakra can quickly restore life-energy throughout the body, creating a sense of calm, relaxation and the confidence to be able to make positive changes. Love is the open, expansive expression of the heart chakra when balanced.

The heart is nowadays associated with the emotions, but in the past it was thought to be the seat of the mind and the soul. This chakra balances our internal reality with the outside world, so is concerned with relationships of all kinds, especially how personal desires and growth can find an outlet via interactions with others.

Feelings of being trapped, the inability to escape from life circumstances and a loss of hope

▲ BALANCING THE HEART CHAKRA WILL HELP TO RESOLVE EMOTIONAL ISSUES AND CLARIFY DIRECTION IN LIFE.

CRYSTALS FOR THE HEART CHAKRA

• GREEN AVENTURINE is an excellent heart balancer and encourages easy expression of the emotions.

• MALACHITE helps dig out deep feelings and hurts, and can break unwanted ties and patterns of behaviour.

• AMAZONITE calms and balances the emotions and helps with throat and lung problems.

• MOSS AGATE is an ideal crystal for supporting the lungs and easing breathing difficulties, and feelings of being emotionally stifled.

• BLOODSTONE is a green quartz flecked with red jasper, giving it an active balance of energy and calm. It stimulates emotional growth while also aiding circulation of the blood.

• PERIDOT is a vivid light green crystal and a good cleanser of the subtle bodies, enabling us to initiate necessary change in our lives and encouraging personal growth.

• EMERALD is a green type of the mineral beryl and is useful in guiding us to a personal direction for growth, bringing clarity to the heart and emotions.

# The solar plexus chakra

**The solar plexus chakra establishes us in our own sense of personal power. It is the power station of the body, physically related to the nervous, digestive and immune systems. The governing colour is yellow.**

Major nerve centres are also found within the solar plexus. The ability to recognize and deal appropriately with energy of all kinds is the function of the solar plexus chakra. Information and control are the sources of all power. So an efficiently functioning solar plexus chakra imbues the individual with a sense of personal confidence, courage, optimism and ability to make the right decisions in any situation.

The solar plexus chakra and its related minor energy centres occupy the area below the ribcage and above the navel. Physically, this area of the body contains the digestive system enabling us to break down and assimilate nutrients from our food. Important organs such as the spleen are found here that sustain our immune system, protecting the body from dangerous micro-organisms in the outside world.

Since life in most modern societies is complex and demanding, as well as subject to many polluting influences, the solar plexus chakra can become overwhelmed and unbalanced. The result is an accumulation of stress and anxiety, the inability to resist infections, an intolerance to foods, additives and chemicals creating allergies, apathy and a loss of enthusiasm and humour. Mental clarity, memory and the ability to focus clearly and study will also be affected.

CRYSTALS FOR THE SOLAR
PLEXUS CHAKRA

• AMBER is among the best-known
of yellow crystals. Actually a pine
resin, it varies in colour from pale
yellow to a rich orange
brown. It is beneficial
for the nervous
system and in
self-healing
processes.

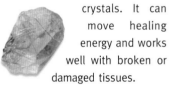

▲ STRESS IS A WELL-KNOWN CAUSE OF MANY
DIGESTIVE PROBLEMS. YELLOW STONES WILL
HELP TENSE MUSCLES TO RELAX.

• RUTILATED QUARTZ is clear or
smoky, and contains fine threads
of golden or orange rutile
crystals. It can
move healing
energy and works
well with broken or
damaged tissues.

• CITRINE QUARTZ can
be bright and
clear yellow
in colour,
and is used
to keep the
mind focused.

• TIGER'S EYE is a yellow and
brown banded form of shiny
quartz, and is used to speed up
energy flow and anchor subtle
changes into the physical body.

• IRON PYRITES, also known
as "fool's gold" because of its
yellow colour, is
able to cleanse
and strengthen,
particularly in
the digestive
system.

# The sacral chakra

**The sacral chakra is located between the navel and the front of the pelvis, the pubic bones. Physically it is related to the reproductive organs and excretory systems. Orange stones naturally balance this chakra.**

The energy of the sacral chakra focuses on sensation, feeling and movement. The exploration of the world and its pleasures and pains are the motivating energy of this centre. All types of creativity begin here. Flow is essential – the flow of curiosity, feelings and information, the fluid that feeds our cells and chemical processes, and the release of toxins from our system – all come under the influence of the sacral chakra. The sacral chakra, when balanced, encourages change and the moving to new adventures. Any form of restriction and rigidity can be helped with orange stones that will restore the natural qualities of the sacral chakra. Blocks of energy anywhere in the body can affect the physical organs and create problems. Infertility and impotence on any level can often be helped by releasing emotional blocks. Stiffness of joints, constipation,

▲ THE SACRAL CHAKRA IS THE WOMB OF ALL CREATIVITY AND THE BIRTH OF EVERY IDEA.

water retention and menstrual difficulties all originate from restricted energy flow. Likewise boredom, indifference or creative blocks indicate that the sacral chakra needs some attention.

CRYSTALS FOR THE SACRAL CHAKRA

• CARNELIAN is a popular orange crystal, and has a sense of warmth and gentle healing energy.

• ORANGE CALCITE offers delicate encouragement of potential, and with its soft and watery feel it can help melt away our problems.

• DARK CITRINE is a balanced and browny-orange stimulator and brings out practical creative skills, as well as being supporting and grounding.

• TOPAZ has elongated crystals and parallel striations, and is a clearing stone that will direct energy around the body.

• COPPER is used, in both nugget and in bracelet forms, to release any stagnation or a lack of flow in our physical and subtle body systems.

Other crystals used at the sacral chakra include ORANGE JASPER, TIGER'S EYE and SUNSTONE.

# The base chakra

Esoterically, this first chakra is the red-coloured root of the lotus, whose thousand petals bloom at the crown. It is the basis and support of our complex physical, mental and subtle system, the source of our primal energy.

The base chakra is situated at the base of the spine and its main functions are to support consciousness within the physical body. All issues to do with survival and protection are focused at this point. The base chakra is concerned with practical skills, the reality of the present moment and the immediate needs of the individual. At a physical level the base chakra relates to all structural systems of

the body, especially the bones. Problems with physical movement, strained ligaments, pulled muscles and misaligned bones can be improved when the base chakra is balanced, as can be complaints affecting the colon, such as diarrhoea or constipation. Lack of

▲ KEEPING THE BODY'S ENERGIES MOVING FREELY AND EFFICIENTLY IS THE TASK OF THE BASE CHAKRA.

energy, fatigue and exhaustion, a loss of interest in life or an excessive interest in spirituality to the detriment of one's well-being, all indicate the need to enhance the life-energy of the base chakra through the use of red stones.

The base chakra is represented in Indian tradition by Ganesha, the elephant god, who guards a person's material wealth and good fortune. Ganesha is also venerated as overseeing the initiation of new projects or new directions in life, especially when taken on the basis of a secure material foundation.

Grounding, motivation and new starts are hence some of the keynotes of the body's first and base chakra. If the base chakra's energy is deep-rooted and strong, the entire chakra system rising from it can also be powerful and effective. It is a two-way conduit of energy in all its forms, both physical and subtle.

Crystals can be placed so that they rest on the ground between the legs, close to the base of the spine. Alternatively, stones can be placed on the top of the legs near to the groin area.

CRYSTALS FOR THE BASE CHAKRA

Among the stones often used at this chakra are:

• GARNET, in its red forms, is an efficient energizer. It can increase energy wherever it is placed and will also activate other stones placed nearby.

• JASPER is a reddish form of quartz, and helps to ground and gently activate the whole body when placed near to the base chakra.

• RUBY is a red variety of carborundum and combines well with energies of the heart centre as well as gently energizing the subtle bodies.

Brown and black crystals can also stabilize and balance the energies of the base chakra.

# CRYSTAL
# TREATMENTS

The therapeutic powers of crystals can be directed through the body to help balance the physical and emotional states, and to heal everyday complaints and ailments ranging from headaches, migraine and menstrual cramps to stress, insomnia and inability to concentrate. The following pages will help you to identify healing crystals and select the appropriate source to ease tension, calm body and mind or boost energy levels.

You will learn how to make gem essences so that you can benefit from a concentrated form of the stone's power. You will also discover how to enhance your surroundings, simply by placing crystals in the appropriate place in your home or work environment.

# Relieving pain

**Crystal healing is by its nature calming and relaxing. Painful conditions often seem to make the body tense itself. This can often prevent the proper flow of healing energy, blood, oxygen and nutrients to where they are needed.**

The placement of crystals naturally begins to ease the imbalances that create pain. By releasing blockages within our subtle bodies, crystals can help stimulate the body's own healing mechanisms to work at a site of tension or pain.

### BACKACHE RELIEF

Lodestone is an old name for magnetic iron ore, which was once used for navigational purposes. Placing one piece near the top of the neck and another at the base of the spine can help to relieve back tensions and stimulate spinal energies.

Help ease back pain with a small, clear quartz at the brow chakra. Imagine a beam of healing white light passing deep into your head with each in-breath.

CLEAR QUARTZ

▼ TO REALIGN THE BODY'S ENERGIES, USE EIGHT PIECES OF TOURMALINE. PLACE TWO AT THE CROWN, TWO MIDWAY ON EACH SIDE, AND TWO AT THE FEET. LIE DOWN AND REST INSIDE THIS CROSS-SHAPED ENERGY PATTERN.

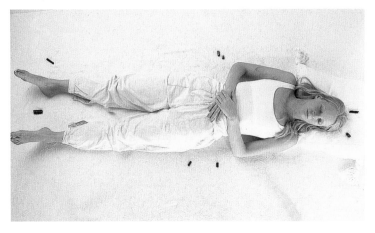

## EASING TENSE MUSCLES

Black or green tourmaline crystals (called also schorl and verdelite) have been found useful where structural adjustment is needed. Knotted muscles can be relieved by placing a piece near them. Neck, jaw or head tension can be eased by wearing earrings made of this stone.

▲ TURQUOISE CAN BE USED WHENEVER THERE IS A NEED FOR CALM, HEALING ENERGY.

▲ MALACHITE, A SOFT MINERAL FORM OF COPPER, IS GOOD AT CALMING PAINFUL AREAS AND DRAWING OUT IMBALANCES.

Malachite is a copper ore that forms in concentric bands of light and dark green. It can calm painful areas and draw out imbalances, but because it absorbs negativity it needs regular cleansing.

Copper can help to reduce inflammations COPPER

and swellings, either in bracelet form or carried as a natural nugget in the pocket.

Turquoise can be placed on the body wherever there is pain, while TURQUOISE carnelian is a powerful healer of the etheric body.

Among pink stones, rose quartz helps to calm aggravated areas and reduce the fears that accompany injury and pain. Placing pink stones at the solar plexus and sacral chakras can help to soothe both mind and body. ROSE QUARTZ

# Soothing headaches

**Headaches tend to occur when there is an imbalance or blockage of energy to the head. Amethyst, with its long tradition as an effective healing stone, can be very useful in soothing headaches.**

All cool-coloured stones (blue, indigo and violet) are useful where there is an energy imbalance resulting in restriction of energy flow and experience of pain. Headaches are notoriously individual in cause and cure. Amethyst, combining the colours of red and blue, is a good crystal to try as it naturally tends to bring balance in any extreme situation.

HEADACHE RELIEF

If a headache can be caught in its early stages it can be a lot easier to reduce the symptoms with crystal healing. First of all, try a simple chakra layout using the appropriate colour stone at each chakra. This will help to stabilize all energy levels in the body.

▼ AMETHYST IS AN ESSENTIAL PART OF YOUR HEALING CRYSTAL COLLECTION.

## HEAD-SOOTHING CRYSTAL LAYOUT

Place one amethyst point on either side of the base of the neck, just above the collar bones, pointing upwards. Place a third stone, also pointing upwards, on the centre of the forehead. A fourth may be added if desired at the top of the head. This placing brings the throat, brow and crown chakras into powerful harmony.

Another common cause of headaches is an imbalance between the head energy and that at the solar plexus, often the result of stress or unsuitable food. If you have a headache and an upset stomach, for example, use a stone that will also balance the solar plexus, such as ametrine.

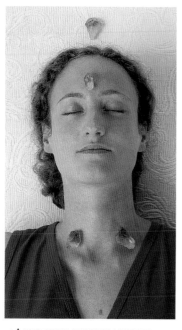

▲ A FOUR-STONE AMETHYST LAYOUT TO SOOTHE HEADACHES.

▶ VIOLET STONES SUCH AS AMETHYST, FLUORITE AND SUGILITE HAVE A NATURAL AFFINITY TO THE CROWN CHAKRA. HELD OR PLACED UPON THE FOREHEAD, THEY COMBINE THE GROUNDING EFFECTS OF RED WITH THE MORE EXPANSIVE QUALITIES OF BLUE TO PROMOTE THE FLOW OF PEACE.

# Easing menstrual problems

**PMS and menstrual cramps are often made worse by physical and emotional tensions, which restrict the body's natural energy flows. Moonstones and opal are among the stones recommended for easing these tensions.**

### CALMING THE EMOTIONS

Moonstone helps in balancing and relaxing emotional states, and also works beneficially on all fluid systems of the body, relieving pain in the abdominal area. Traditional Ayurvedic texts in India state that moonstone is the ideal stone for women to wear, and indeed, it can be made into charming jewellery.

DARK OPALS

MOONSTONES

### RELIEVING STOMACH CRAMPS

Dark opal is similar in properties to moonstone, acting powerfully at the first and second chakras to ease menstrual cramps in a short time. Place a small piece in a hip or trouser pocket.

To reinforce chakra healing for PMS, carry with you a dark opal or an orange stone, such as carnelian, associated with the sacral chakra. When you have the chance, rub the stone lightly across your lower abdomen, from just below the navel, making a large circle to the left, and allowing it to spiral towards the middle. Feel the warmth of the crystal's energy flowing into you from the stone and the easing of tension that this brings.

CARNELIAN

### Five-moonstone pattern

A healing pattern of five moonstones amplifies the relaxing and therapeutic potential of the stone to ease physical and emotional tensions. Lying down comfortably, position one stone at the top of your head, one near each armpit and one on each hip.

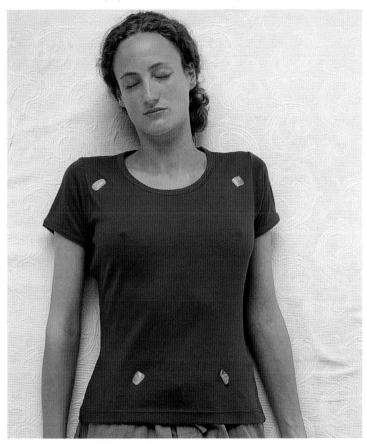

▲ FIND A COMFORTABLE POSITION IN WHICH TO LIE DOWN, CLOSE YOUR EYES AND ALLOW THE FIVE-MOONSTONE PATTERN TO EASE AWAY ANY MENSTRUAL TENSIONS WITHIN YOUR BODY.

# Energizing crystals

**Sometimes poor energy is simply caused by a temporary imbalance in the chakra system, especially the base and solar plexus. Redistribution of natural energy reserves can help to revitalize depleted areas, and restore vitality.**

Red, orange and yellow stones, such as garnet, amber and topaz, can promote increased energy. Yellow citrine makes a wonderful substitute for summer sun on a dull winter's day.

More earthy tones, such as tiger's eye, dark citrine and jasper, can help you focus on practical action to be taken.

▲ FOR A QUICK ENERGY BOOST TO THE WHOLE SYSTEM, HOLD A CLEAR QUARTZ CRYSTAL, POINT UPWARDS, IN EACH HAND, AND PLACE A LARGE CITRINE STONE AT THE SOLAR PLEXUS.

GARNET

AMBER

TOPAZ

JASPER

TIGER'S EYE

CITRINE

DARK CITRINE

# Aiding concentration

**The natural, organized structure of a crystal lattice automatically increases the clarity and orderliness of a study area or workplace. A beautiful clear crystal such as quartz can bring stillness and focus to the mind.**

Yellow is known to stimulate the logical functions of the mind, so a bright yellow amber, citrine or fluorite will assist your memory and recall. Fluorite is particularly good as it helps balance the working of the brain hemispheres.

Deep blue stones, such as kyanite, sodalite and sapphire, will encourage your communication skills and a better understanding of ideas and concepts.

▲ KEEP A FAVOURITE CRYSTAL NEAR YOU AS YOU STUDY, AND TAKE IT WITH YOU TO AN EXAM FOR EXTRA CONFIDENCE AND CLARITY.

CITRINE

FLUORITE

SODALITE

KYANITE

AMBER

SAPPHIRE

# Releasing stress

**A shock, accident or loss may leave you shaken and vulnerable. Look out for stress symptoms, such as tensing of muscles, recurrent mental replays of events and sudden welling up of emotions.**

CALMING LAYOUT

The effects of stress can be released by this layout. Continue regularly until the stress eases.

**1** Place a rose quartz at the heart chakra, with four quartz points facing outwards, positioned diagonally around it.

**2** At the sacral chakra, below the navel, place a tiger's eye, and surround it with another four quartz points, facing inwards and also placed diagonally around it.

**3** The stones at the heart release emotional tension, while those on the abdomen balance the chakras above and give grounded energy and stability.

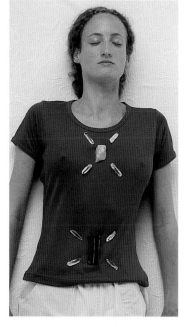

▲ YOU WILL NEED EIGHT SMALL, CLEAR QUARTZ CRYSTALS, A ROSE QUARTZ AND A TIGER'S EYE.

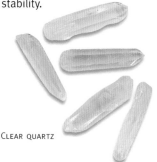

CLEAR QUARTZ

ROSE QUARTZ

TIGER'S EYE

# Calming crystals

Here is a calming crystal layout to help during times of emotional stress to restore calm and equilibrium. Signs of stress being released include muscle twitches, deep breaths or sighs, yawning and watery eyes.

SOOTHING CRYSTAL LAYOUT

**1** Place a rose quartz at the heart chakra, surrounded by four quartz points in a cross formation. Points should be facing outwards to remove emotional imbalances; or set points facing inwards to stabilize an over-emotional state.

**2** Position a citrine stone at the solar plexus chakra, with its darker point facing downwards. This increases the sense of security and feeling of safety.

**3** Place an amethyst on the third eye chakra to calm the mind. If the release is found to be too strong, remove stones from the heart area and place a hand over the solar plexus.

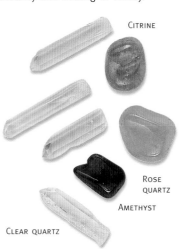

CITRINE

ROSE QUARTZ

AMETHYST

CLEAR QUARTZ

▲ FOR A CALMING LAYOUT USE FOUR CLEAR QUARTZ CRYSTALS, A ROSE QUARTZ, A CITRINE AND AN AMETHYST.

# Aiding restful sleep

**Taking crystals to bed is an easy and comforting way of dealing with insomnia. Experiment with different crystals for different types of sleeplessness. Hold the stones, put them on or under your pillow or near to you as you settle.**

DEALING WITH SLEEPLESS NIGHTS
Chrysoprase, an apple green form of chalcedony quartz, has been found in many cases to encourage peaceful sleep. Place a stone under your pillow or by your bedside table.

If tension or worry is the cause of restlessness, try amethyst, rose quartz or citrine.

If something you have eaten is disturbing your sleep pattern, a digestive calmer such as ametrine, moonstone or iron pyrites may work for you.

▲ HOLD THE APPROPRIATE STONES OR HAVE THEM NEARBY AS YOU SLEEP.

CHRYSOPRASE

AMETHYST

CITRINE

ROSE QUARTZ

IRON PYRITES

AMETRINE

## BANISHING BAD DREAMS

Where there is fear, particularly related to bad dreams, place a grounding and protecting stone, such as tourmaline, staurolite or smoky quartz, at the bottom of the bed. Labradorite can also help chase away unwelcome thoughts or feelings.

A stronger energy might be needed to counter nightmares: place a large, smooth moss agate or tektite by the bed where you can touch it and feel its reassuring solidity.

STAUROLITE

TOURMALINE

SMOKY QUARTZ

MOSS AGATE

▼ IF TENSION AND WORRY ARE THE CAUSES OF RESTLESSNESS TRY PLACING ROSE QUARTZ, AMETHYST OR CITRINE BY YOUR PILLOW.

# Crystal essences

**You can benefit from the healing properties of gems by making your own crystal essences. These are vibrational preparations made by immersing gemstones in spring water and exposing to direct sunlight.**

Gem essences are believed to work by allowing the energy pattern of a chosen stone to be imprinted on the water. Sunlight is best for this process, but leaving a stone in water by your bedside overnight and drinking the water first thing in the morning can also be beneficial. Remove the stone before using the essence.

The charged water can be drunk on the spot or bottled for later use in helping the healing processes of the body. It is not necessary to ingest a gem essence in order for it to be effective. Rubbing a few drops on pulse points or around a chakra area, or close to an area of imbalance can work just as well. Keep crystal essence bottles in the refrigerator and try to drink them within one week. You should not freeze them. Fresh-made essence is usually best. You can also spray indoor plants or add the essence water to your bath.

Caution: some stones are toxic or dissolve in water (crystals of salt, for example). Gem water made from the quartz family is safe. Try citrine, amethyst or tiger's eye.

◀ DRINKING A HOME-MADE CRYSTAL ESSENCE, SUCH AS THIS ONE MADE BY PLACING AN AMETHYST IN CLEAR SPRING WATER, GIVES YOU A CONCENTRATED FORM OF YOUR STONE'S HEALING POWER.

## MAKING A MOONSTONE ESSENCE

A moonstone essence has the ability to calm our emotions. Moonstone is soft and cooling, because of its feminine orientation.

**1** Take a cleansed gemstone and place it into a clear glass bowl. Fill the bowl with fresh spring water until the stone is covered.

**2** Leave the bowl outside under the light of a full moon for three hours, or overnight if the night is calm and clear.

**3** Remove the moonstone, remembering to cleanse it after use, and pour the liquid into a clear glass.

**4** Take a drink of the moonstone infusion first thing in the morning in order to prepare yourself for a harmonious day.

# Enhancing your home

Crystals can make attractive decorations for the home and they can also enhance the surroundings by bringing a balancing and cleansing influence on many levels, helping to neutralize emotional debris and pollution.

▲ Adding crystals to a sacred space keeps the energies fresh and positive.

Crystals can create a sacred space in your home, as a simple quiet place in which to rest or as an elaborate altar with sacred images. Honour an anniversary or guest with a temporary special space or set aside a permanent meditative area in your home or garden.

Make a crystal lightbox by placing a large transparent or translucent stone in front of a light source. Change the mood by using a yellow crystal for relaxation, red for energy and violet for mystery.

▶ Crystals with internal fractures or rainbows, such as rutilated quartz or moss agate, can make beautiful lights.

◄ CRYSTALS IN AN AQUARIUM REVEAL THEIR VIVID COLOURS, AND ALSO ENERGIZE THE SURROUNDINGS.

▲ CREATE A MINI ZEN GARDEN BY FILLING A FLAT BOWL WITH CLEAN SAND OR DRY GRAVEL. ARRANGE INTERESTING STONES AND CRYSTALS ON IT, AND USE A COMB OR FORK TO DRAW PATTERNS IN THE SAND.

Pets can be treated with gems and crystals, both to maintain health and when they are unwell. Use a crystal pendulum to balance the energy in four-footed animals, or place crystals safely around a sleeping area. Energizing water can be dropped on your fingers and then stroked through the fur of a cat or dog. A small gemstone can be attached to a dog or cat collar. Sick animals may find the presence of a crystal in their basket or hutch comforting.

A quiet corner of the garden is a good place for reflection, and crystals placed near the plants keep them healthy too. House plants benefit from crystals placed in their soil, quartz and emerald (gem quality is not necessary) are popular. Aquamarine and jade are also said to enhance plant energies, while turquoise can help plants recover from damage and disease.

▲ A QUARTZ CRYSTAL WILL ENHANCE A HOUSE PLANT'S OVERALL HEALTH.

enhancing your home **111**

# Crystals in the workplace

**Whether you work at home or in the office, crystals can be used to enhance your working area in simple, effective ways. Consider the factors you would most like to improve and select the types of colour and crystal that might help.**

If you work in an office or factory, there is much you can do to make your personal space a pleasing place to be:

• Keep natural stones or crystals as paperweights or as dividers in a file or bookcase.

• Use carved stone pots or bowls on the desk as containers in which to store pens or paperclips.

• Place stones on the soil of potted plants in your work area.

• Have a favourite crystal as a "worry stone" for your pocket. The telephone and computer can be particular causes of tension and stress, demanding our attention and raising the body's adrenaline levels when emotions are triggered.

▶ KEEP A SMALL BOWL OF STONES NEAR THE PHONE AS A FOCUS FOR YOUR ATTENTION. IT WILL ALSO HELP AVOID UNNECESSARY DEPLETION OF YOUR ENERGY BY BECOMING OVERLY INVOLVED IN OTHER PEOPLE'S PROBLEMS.

Moonstone helps to foster understanding of our colleagues' points of view and, as such, is an excellent aid to communication. It also acts to balance our emotional states and clear away tensions, and restores the balance of the body's fluid systems.

Obsidian is a form of black volcanic glass, often with white flecks (snowflake obsidian), patches of dark red (mahogany obsidian) or a smoky translucence (Apache tears). It is known as a good aid to concentration, working patiently to bring imbalances to the surface and reveal hidden factors

SNOWFLAKE OBSIDIAN

▲ OFFSET THE STRONG ELECTROMAGNETIC FIELDS CREATED BY COMPUTER SCREENS BY PUTTING A CRYSTAL ON THE MONITOR OR NEAR IT. CLEAR QUARTZ IS RECOMMENDED, BUT IT MUST BE CLEANSED FREQUENTLY.

surrounding a situation. Other stones can then assist by clearing away this clutter, leaving the mind clear and focused.

Fluorite is also found in a variety of colours, with violet or mauve among the most frequent. Its presence can help in a work environment through its capacity to release dynamic or inspirational ideas, as it is associated with the crown chakra and acts as a link between subtle and practical aspects of consciousness.

FLUORITE

# Crystal colours directory

 We have seen how coloured crystals are associated with the chakra system, and how they work in many different types of healing. This directory looks briefly at the most commonly used crystals according to their colours.

DIRECTORY OF COLOURED CRYSTALS

Note that some crystals are listed below under several colours. The colour categories are rarely exact in practice, and good stones can be a little or widely different from the suggested match.

This variety and individuality, however, is part of the attraction of choosing crystals. Finding a stone that resonates to your own vibration is the beginning of your healing experience.

| | |
|---|---|
| RED | garnet, jasper, ruby, red tiger's eye, carnelian. |
| ORANGE | carnelian, orange calcite, dark citrine, topaz, copper, sunstone. |
| YELLOW | amber, rutilated quartz, tiger's eye, citrine quartz, iron pyrites, yellow topaz. |
| GREEN | green aventurine, malachite, bloodstone, amazonite, moss agate, peridot, emerald, jade. |
| BLUE | aquamarine, turquoise, blue lace agate, celestite, sapphire, sodalite. |
| INDIGO | lapis lazuli, sodalite, kyanite, azurite, sapphire. |
| VIOLET | amethyst, fluorite, sugilite, iolite, kunzite, charoite. |
| WHITE | clear quartz, herkimer diamond, Iceland spa, moonstone, selenite. |
| BLACK | smoky quartz, obsidian, tourmaline, haematite. |
| PINK | rose quartz, rhodonite, kunzite, rhodocrosite. |
| MULTICOLOURED | opal, azurite-malachite, labradorite, hawk's eye, ametrine. |

## Quartz: the family that has everything

There is one remarkable family of crystals that on its own encompasses most of the colours and healing opportunities of the spectrum. As such, it deserves a special mention in any study of crystals.

QUARTZ is probably one of the commonest minerals on Earth, being composed of the abundant elements silica and oxygen. Stones in the quartz family may be bright, clear and simple or dark, dense and complex, depending on the heat and pressure involved in their formation. Colours and forms vary widely because the crystal lattice allows other atoms to enter at a microscopic level. These often alter the way that light passes through them, changing the visible colour.

CLEAR QUARTZ is colourless and shiny; MILKY QUARTZ is white, as is OPAL (the high water content creating a display of flashing colour); ROSE QUARTZ is pink and translucent, while CARNELIAN is orange and JASPER is often red, but also yellow, green and blue; RUTILATED QUARTZ is golden yellow and CITRINE ranges from yellow to orange-brown; CHRYSOPRASE is bright apple-green and AVENTURINE is green or blue, with tiny sparks of mica or pyrites; in the blue range are the delicate BLUE LACE AGATE

and dreamy purple AMETHYST; among the mixed colours are the agates, with wavy parallel coloured bands, including MOSS AGATE and BANDED AGATE, and TIGER'S EYE, with subtle browns, yellows, blue and red; at the darkest end of the spectrum are SMOKY QUARTZ, BLOODSTONE, or HELIOTROPE, in a dark, shiny green, TOURMALINE QUARTZ, embedded with fine black needles and onyx, with its straight lines of white on black.

# HEALING WITH
# COLOUR

The vast majority of us spend our lives surrounded by colour, but few of us pause to think about its impact on our psyche. On a purely instinctive level, the colour of the clothes we wear, the foods we eat or the paints and furnishings we use to decorate our home reflect our mood and emotions. This is colour healing in its simplest form.

By exploring the subject a little further, we can also use colour healing to cure discomfort, or to create a specific atmosphere to actually enhance the purpose of a room, and make it a playground for a range of emotions. So, go ahead – follow your instinct and find out how simple colour appreciation enables you to optimize well-being.

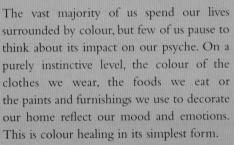

# Life in colour

**You are swamped with colour from the moment you are born: it is an aspect of everything you eat, drink, touch and are surrounded by. You can use colours to depict your health, attitudes, emotions – even psychic experiences.**

Nearly everyone takes colour for granted most of the time, but it is impossible to be indifferent to it. Colour affects every environment: at home, at work, at school, in the city or in the countryside. The colours of the clothes you wear affect your mood and reflect your personality, which in turn influences other people's perception of you and so affects your relationships.

Colour helps you to determine when fruits are ripe. Your skin changes colour with shock, shyness or excitement. Too much yellow light can cause arguments between people, and blue light can quieten them. Colour constantly enriches your life, whether it is the green of grass or trees, deep blue sky, a purple and gold sunset, or a beautiful rainbow.

Without light there is no life, and no growth. A plant deprived of light will soon wither and die and living beings are continually reacting to the wide range of stimuli called light. From light come all the colours, each with its own impact upon living systems. Light is energy, and all energy acts upon everything with which it comes into contact. What you see as colour is simply the brain's way of recognizing the different energy qualities of light.

Many healing needs can be met by the use of colour to bring about harmony and balance within the psyche and the body. The invisible vibrations of colour

◀ CHILDREN ARE ATTRACTED BY THE STRENGTH OF BRIGHT COLOURS.

▲ Colour enriches your life. Many cultures use bright colours when celebrating special occasions.

can either relax or stimulate, according to the colours chosen for healing. Its power is both transcendent and intuitive, and there are several ways of harnessing it for health and well-being. Colour does more than just please the eye. You can eat it, drink it, and wear appropriately coloured clothes or jewellery, absorbing the colour through your skin as well as your eyes. Your home can be a haven of health and peace when you furnish it in colours appropriate to your needs and aspirations.

Disease is often regarded as an enemy, but think of it as your friend. It is telling you the truth about yourself, and the ways in which you are out of harmony with the "real" you. Working with colour and understanding the connection between yourself and colour offers a key to good health and vitality.

Although colour healing can be very effective, it should not replace any medical treatment. If the symptoms persist or worsen, consult a health professional.

▼ The beautiful colours of the sunset are joyous and calming.

# The evolution of colour healing

**Ancient cultures worshipped the sun – whence all light, and all colour, comes – and were aware of its healing powers. The therapeutic use of colour can be traced in the teachings attributed to the Egyptian god Thoth.**

EARLY COLOUR THERAPY

Following the ancient teachings, Egyptian and Greek physicians – including Hippocrates, the father of Western medicine – used different coloured ointments and salves as remedies, and practised in treatment rooms painted in healing shades. In 1st-century Rome, the physician Aulus Cornelius Celsus wrote about the therapeutic use of colour, but with the coming of Christianity such ancient wisdom came to be associated with pagan beliefs and was disallowed by the Church.

In the 9th century the Arab physician Avicenna systematized the teachings of Hippocrates. He wrote about colour as a symptom of disease and as a treatment, suggesting, for example, that red would act as a stimulant on blood flow while yellow could reduce pain and inflammation. However, by the 18th century philosophers and scientists were more concerned with the material world, and insisted on visible proof of scientific theories.

▼ THE ANCIENT EGYPTIANS KNEW ABOUT THE HEALING PROPERTIES OF COLOURS.

◀ BATHE YOURSELF IN A NATURAL GREEN VIBRATION TO INSTIL POSITIVE THOUGHTS AND CREATIVITY.

establishment's continued scepticism, therapists have since developed the use of colour in both psychological testing and physical diagnosis. The Lüscher Colour Test is based on the theory that colours stimulate different parts of the autonomic nervous system, affecting metabolic rate and glandular secretions, and studies in the 1950s showed that yellow and red light raised blood pressure while blue light tended to lower it. The use of blue light to treat neonatal jaundice is now common practice, and it has also been effective as pain relief in cases of rheumatoid arthritis.

Advances in medicine focused on surgery and drugs, and less quantifiable healing techniques that dealt with spiritual and mental well-being were rejected.

## COLOUR THERAPY REDISCOVERED

In 1878 Edwin Babbitt published *The Principles of Light and Colour* and achieved world renown with his comprehensive theory, prescribing colours for a range of conditions. Despite the medical

▶ GREEN, TURQUOISE AND BLUE OBJECTS HAVE A TRANQUIL AIR.

the evolution of colour healing **121**

# Natural colour

**From forests to cities, people adapt to the unique qualities of their surroundings. Colour creates the ambience of a place because the vibrational energy of colour operates directly on your energy levels and emotions.**

### THE CALM OF NATURE

Most people experience a lifting of mood on a woodland walk as the green of nature fills their vision. The effects of colour can be felt when relaxing by the sea in summer, the predominant colours being the blues of the sea and sky, which generate a feeling of expansiveness and peace.

Turquoise is an important colour that tempers the deeper blues with an extra sense of calmness and comfort. The golden yellow of sand and sunlight energizes and balances the body's systems, reducing anxiety and stress levels.

▲ THE STRIKING COLOURS OF THE PEACOCK'S TAIL FEATHERS ACT AS A TERRITORIAL WARNING SIGNAL TO ITS COMPETITORS.

### THE SEEING WORLD

Full colour vision is a rare development in the animal world; it occurs in the higher vertebrates – including humans – as well as a few unexpected animals, such as the tortoise and the octopus.

Striking colour displays are used by many animals, such as the peacock, to attract mates or to deter enemies. Using colour as camouflage is also common. The squid has a complex language of expression, sending waves of colours across its body.

◀ THE BLUE OF THE SEA IS ONE OF THE MOST SOOTHING COLOURS OF ALL.

# Colours in different cultures

**Colour is an intrinsic part of human life, and although the physical effects of colour are biologically constant, its psychological interpretation and symbolism can vary when it forms part of a cultural language.**

RED

In Tibetan and some pagan traditions, red is the colour of the female sun, white the male moon. The two symbolize the union of opposites: the power of creation. Red can also be associated with the male, for example Santa Claus, who also retains the symbolism of the Arctic shaman bringing healing and gifts to his people.

GREEN

In the Western tradition, green is associated with wild nature, the power of growth and uncultivated space inhabited by spirits, elves

▼ IN TIBET, RED IS A COLOUR ASSOCIATED WITH CREATIVITY, PRAYER AND HEALING.

▲ WHITE CAN BE SYMBOLIC OF PURITY AND INNOCENCE, AND SO IT IS OFTEN CHOSEN AS THE COLOUR FOR BRIDAL WEAR.

and fairies. In the world of Islam, the colour green is sacred. In a landscape dominated by arid wilderness, green represents the oasis, the sign of life, water and shelter: the symbol of paradise.

BLACK AND WHITE

In much of Europe death has been associated with black. In China, however, white is seen as the colour of winter, when all things return to a dormant state, so mourners wear white. Chinese people tend to avoid wearing white in everyday life because it reminds them of a shroud, whereas in the West white is associated simply with purity.

# Colour at home

**Colour is a sensation that enriches the world: there is no better way to use it than by harnessing its strength and benefits to enhance your home. Blending colours successfully can help to create a harmonious atmosphere.**

## WELCOMING THE SUN

When you are creating your home environment, take into consideration the amount of sunlight in each room. It is important that the glow from the sun's beams is received into your psyche, for its purifying effect. Allowing sunlight to flood into dark corners also rids a room of its staleness and kills some bacteria.

When you are decorating, think about the effects of colour, how the room will be used, and also about the people who will use it: do they have any problems that could be alleviated or worsened by your colour choices? What are their ambitions and aims?

## COLOUR AND SIZE

Take into consideration the size and shape of each room: the stronger the colour, the smaller a room will seem. Small rooms tend to look more spacious decorated in single pale colours. Colours become more intense in larger areas, and a strong colour can enclose a room, causing claustrophobia. Dark narrow rooms need light, clear colours.

Check how much daylight the space gets before using white, as a bright white room can be tiring for the eyes and cause frustration. Deep colours may look good with the sun on them; they become several shades duller at night in artificial light, but can look cosy if firelight or candlelight are used. If you are painting only one wall in a different colour, do not choose a wall where there is a door or window as this dissipates the colour energy.

◀ AN ORANGE ROOM WILL INSTIL CHEERFULNESS INTO ITS OCCUPANTS.

# ROOM-BY-ROOM GUIDE TO COLOUR

The colours of your home should suit not only the function of each room, but should also be used to create harmony. Use coloured flowers or ornaments for particular occasions to influence the atmosphere.

Entrance hall: To welcome your guests include warm colours, such as the range of reds.  Or to create a sense of space choose softer pastel shades.

Kitchen: Too much green may slow you down just when you need to be active, but a touch of yellow inspires efficiency.

 Living room: Yellow puts people in a good humour; add brown to give a sense of security.

Dining room: Include a hint of silver at a dinner party. It aids digestion and is uplifting – adding sparkle to guests' conversations.

Bedroom: Calming blue is a perfect colour for the bedroom. A touch of indigo can also help if  you suffer from headaches or insomnia. Stimulating red may cause sleeplessness, so avoid.

Bathroom: Hints of pale green will soothe and feed a tired nervous system.

# Colour at work

**Until quite recently, coloured decor for offices was almost unthinkable. Sterile white, grey or drab browns were the norm. Today, the trend is to make the most of the effect that colour has on people and the ambience it can create.**

### THE EFFECT OF COLOUR

Promoting the effective use of colour in the office is important both for the comfort of the employees and the productivity of the business. If thoughtlessly applied, colour can interfere and distract from work. If only white is used it can cause frustration. Blue creates an atmosphere of calm and is good for creativity. Brown creates tiredness and lethargy and grey induces depression and melancholy. If you use beige, add green or rose pink to alleviate the negative slackness that it can bring to the room.

Don't forget details such as company stationery, as it also makes a colour statement. You could change from white paper to a shade that may better reflect your company's image.

### THE CITY OFFICE

Offices in which activity is high, in areas such as sales and banking, should use red upholstery. This definitely puts workers in the hot seat and adds impetus and drive to their performance. Add green walls, to counteract the red and reduce headaches that are brought on by the pressure of work.

◄ BLUE IN THE STUDY AREA CREATES A SENSE OF CALM AND CAN INSPIRE THE WRITER.

▶ In city offices with little natural daylight and only limited scope for individuality, using colour to energize and personalize space becomes a priority.

### The executive office

When you are the boss you need an office where employees and directors can talk to you and be reminded that you lead the way. A purple carpet gives an impression of big ideas and creativity along with luxury and authority. Touches of gold encourage feelings of trust and loyalty, but don't forget to add healthy green plants to represent money and to balance power and character.

### The open-plan office

When choosing colours for a large office, you would be well advised to make the overall decor a basic cream and introduce touches of brighter colours, such as orange, emerald green, rose and rich blue. If only one accent colour can be used, choose a bright turquoise as this will help to give a greater sense of privacy.

### The home office

An office at home can encourage the workaholic. An effective combination would be a royal blue carpet with yellow curtains and pale blue or primrose yellow walls: this should succeed in keeping the business in the office only, and not allow work to penetrate into your personal life.

◀ Green in the office will help to generate abundance and make money.

# Light waves and colour

**Visible light is a small portion of the electromagnetic spectrum, which also includes ultraviolet and infrared light. These last two are just beyond the vision of humans, but can still have an effect on our health.**

LIGHT WAVES

The distance between the two crests of a wave (the wavelength) determines what type of wave it is. Radio waves are very long; cosmic rays are very short. Around the middle of the spectrum is the tiny portion we experience as visible light. Within this, further gradations produce different colours. The longest waves are at the red end of the spectrum, and the shortest waves are at the purple end, with those of the other colours falling in between. Colour therapists often refer to pure colours as "rays".

◄ WHITE LIGHT REFRACTED THROUGH A PRISM REVEALS ITS COMPONENT COLOURS – THE FULL RAINBOW SPECTRUM.

WHAT IS COLOUR?

A coloured surface absorbs or reflects certain wavelengths of light. A red flower absorbs all light striking it except the red end of the spectrum, which is reflected. A white surface reflects all light that hits it, while a black surface absorbs it all.

The emotional and physiological response of humans to colour is profound: even people without sight will identify warm and cool colours. The stimulating effects of reds and oranges and the calming qualities of blues and violets, for example, are linked to the biological triggers of daylight and nightfall, and these responses are harnessed as part of the colour healing process.

◄ A RAINBOW IS WHITE LIGHT REFRACTED OR SEPARATED INTO ITS COMPONENT COLOURS.

# Sense of sight

**Colour has been shown to initiate profound changes in the nervous system. The eyes allow the light energy of colour to be carried to the centre of the brain, influencing cellular function, physical activity, emotional and mental states.**

## THE EYE

The human eye is a sophisticated sensing device. Light passes through the transparent lens and stimulates the specialized light-sensitive cells in the retina at the back of the eyeball. These send electrical impulses via the optic nerve into the brain to be interpreted. The process of vision is primarily a function of the brain, for the eyes "see" only a small area at any one time. The eyeballs move very rapidly across the field of vision, 50–70 times a second, and the visual part of the brain makes sense of all the information.

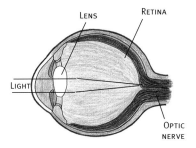

▲ LIGHT ENTERS THE EYE, TRIGGERING THE NERVES IN THE LIGHT-SENSITIVE CELLS IN THE RETINA, WHICH THEN LINK UP TO THE BRAIN.

## COLOUR AND THE BRAIN

Nerves go directly from the retina to the hypothalamus and pituitary gland (both are parts of the brain), which control most of the body's life-sustaining functions, and modify behaviour patterns and regulate energy levels. Thus the application of light can directly influence the body.

In addition, specialist cells within the skin have a sensitivity to light and so this is a second area in which your body can be directly influenced by colour.

◄ SOME CREATURES CAN SEE A WIDER SPECTRUM OF COLOURS THAN HUMANS.

# The psychology of colour

**Colour can affect your personality whether this is due to cultural conditioning or personal associations. If you were wearing blue on a very happy occasion, for example, the colour may continue to remind you of that experience.**

## COLOUR AND MOOD

There are psychological associations with each colour, and colours can be linked with moods. Reds, oranges and yellows are warm and expansive and give a feeling of energy, excitement and joy. Blues, indigos and purples are calming and cool. They quieten the temperament and induce relaxation. The psychology of colour is a language that you can learn, just as you can learn to read and write. When you understand the basic meanings of colours you can choose the colours in your life according to your needs.

▲ THE SUNSET COLOURS, PINK AND GOLD, ARE NURTURING AND EXCELLENT FOR HEALING EMOTIONAL TRAUMA.

## RESTORING BALANCE

Each colour vibrates at a distinctive rate that corresponds with a part of the body. When you are well you may like most colours, but illness will bring out preferences for specific colours. It is these that are needed for healing. When you are exhausted you may be drawn to reds. Some-one who is over-excited would benefit from blues, but depression needs yellows and golds.

The following guide will help you to explore how you feel, and help you to choose colours to enhance your well-being.

◀ RED IS THE COLOUR ASSOCIATED WITH ADVENTURE SPORTS SUCH AS SKI-ING.

# Chakras and colour

**Ancient texts describe seven energy centres, or chakras, arranged along the spinal column. Each one focuses energy, and each is associated with a colour. They are forever changing and balancing to preserve your well-being.**

WORKING WITH CHAKRAS

Every individual has a particular chakra pattern, some being more dominant than others. This can lead to an energy imbalance, so you will need to determine which chakras need balancing. In this way you will be able to maintain a harmonious and healthy state.

Colour therapy is a technique that can work directly with chakras. Shining coloured light on the chakra, over the whole body or through the eyes all create

physical, emotional and mental changes which re-balance the chakras. If coloured light is not easily available, visualizing the necessary colours can also work.

## THE SEVEN CHAKRAS

CROWN CHAKRA: purple
Overall balance, intuition.
Linked to pineal gland.

BROW CHAKRA: indigo
Understanding, perception.
Linked to pituitary gland.

THROAT CHAKRA: blue
Communication, expression.
Linked to thyroid glands.

HEART CHAKRA: green
Relationships, development.
Linked to heart and thymus.

SOLAR PLEXUS CHAKRA: yellow
Sense of identity, confidence.
Linked to pancreas and spleen.

SACRAL CHAKRA: orange
Creativity, feelings, sex drive.
Linked to adrenal glands.

BASE CHAKRA: red
Survival, stability, practicality.
Linked to gonads.

▼ THE POSITION AND COLOUR OF CHAKRAS (ENERGY CENTRES) ON THE BODY.

# The energy of brilliance

**Brilliance represents the universal intelligence and its source is the sun. Created when all rays of colour come together in perfect balance, it is the light from which all colours spring: the light seen in near-death experiences.**

## THE CHARACTER OF BRILLIANCE

Brilliance itself is not a colour: it is the original or cosmic light. Add a touch of brilliance to any colour and it will become brighter. Without brilliance there can be no vision. Brilliance cuts directly through to the truth. It is the hard light that exposes all flaws and

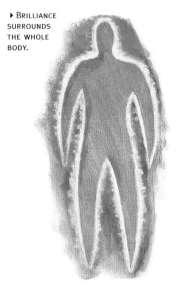

▶ BRILLIANCE SURROUNDS THE WHOLE BODY.

corruption. It contains the essence of all qualities, both positive and negative, sparkling in the brilliance of perfection. It clears the way for necessary actions. Brilliance clears any cloudiness in a person or over-dominance of any one colour. To recharge yourself at any time simply visualize pure brilliant

◀ BATHING IN A WATERFALL IS LIKE STANDING IN A CASCADE OF BRILLIANT LIGHT.

▶ This arrangement of six clear crystals is called the Seal of Solomon. It will quieten your mind and inspire brilliant insights.

light. When you say that someone is "brilliant", you are really acknowledging his or her purity of vision and action.

### BRILLIANCE AND THE BODY

The lymphatic system and the tissues that filter out the debris from the body relate to brilliance. Crystal clear water is pure liquid brilliance: bathing in a waterfall is the equivalent of standing under a cascade of clear light. Another

## WHEN BRILLIANCE CAN HELP

• Brilliance will bring a ray of hope to your life when all seems lost. • It can also bring change, and allows the delusions of your life to dissolve. You will see situations clearly and it will allow you to wipe the slate clean. • Applying brilliance may bring about a move to a new home, a change of job, or a subtle inner transformation. You will find that old patterns fall away and are replaced with new ones, full of joy and an uplifting of the spirit.

way to apply brilliance to yourself is to stand in front of an open window, or to go outside and take a brief sunshine bath: you can renew yourself time and time again.

▶ BRILLIANCE CAPTURED IN CLEAR CRYSTALS INSPIRES CLEAR THOUGHTS.

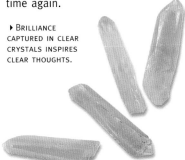

the energy of brilliance **133**

# The energy of red

**Red is the nearest visible light to infrared. It is a fiery force: the spirit of physical life, full of power and drive. It signifies courage and liberation, passion and excitement. Too much red burns, but at the right level it supports life.**

### THE CHARACTER OF RED

When the influence of red is managed well within the system, its energy can be harnessed to motivate people. These are the innovators and entrepreneurs who are full of ideas. They prefer to move from one project to another, getting things started and then moving on.

People under the influence of red are often renowned for their daring exploits and can be somewhat extrovert and boastful about their skills. An overload of red causes restlessness and impatience in those nearby. It can result in selfishness, making people focus on their own needs and survival above everything else. Sometimes this drive to survive is what fuels

▲ A BRIGHT RED SKY AT SUNRISE CAN SIGNIFY THE APPROACH OF A CHANGEABLE AND STORMY WEATHER SYSTEM.

impulsive actions and rash comments. Red at its worst is tyrannical, seeking advancement no matter who or what suffers.

At its best, red will ensure a satisfying and passionate love life. Red brings focus to the physicality of life, to the process of living.

◀ FOR AN EXCITING DAY, DRESS YOUR CHILD IN RED CLOTHES.

## CAUTION
Do not use red lighting in chromotherapy above the waist for heart conditions. Medical advice should be taken regarding any heart problem.

◄ RED IS THE COLOUR OF THE
BASE CHAKRA, THE AREA WHICH
GOVERNS REPRODUCTION.

The colour red is symbolic of what you need to survive. Life should be grabbed and lived with a sense of immediacy. Without red you may become listless and out of touch with reality.

## RED AND THE BODY

Primarily, red is associated with the genitals and reproductive organs. Another area of red focus is the blood and circulation, as it increases the body's ability to absorb iron. Red also prompts adrenalin to release into the bloodstream – hence its link with aggression.

## WHEN RED CAN HELP

• Use red to help circulatory problems, such as cold hands and feet, hardening of the arteries, anaemia and exhaustion. • Red can also be used to treat infertility and is especially good for stiff muscles and joints, particularly in the legs and feet.
• Red is useful in cases of paralysis, and works excellently if also combined with physiotherapy (physical therapy). • Red counteracts shyness and enables you to put your life back into action.

Red is a colour charged with energy and vitality. After an illness, when the body has been weakened, red is excellent for stimulating renewed strengths and encouraging recovery.

◄ THE LAVA FLOW FROM VOLCANOES IS RED. IT IS NATURE'S WARNING SIGNAL FOR DANGER.

the energy of red **135**

# The energy of orange

**As a mixture of red and yellow, orange blends the properties of both colours. Orange energy displays some sense of direction and purpose – it moves along those pathways that fuel its own existence.**

### THE CHARACTER OF ORANGE

Orange has a persistent nature and can be summed up by one word: opportunity. Always one jump ahead, orange has the courage to grasp opportunities as soon as they occur. Orange is a strong colour that dares to trust intuition, tapping into creative resources and allowing skills to develop. The orange personality loves to experiment with new and exciting recipes in the kitchen. They are physical and will be drawn to sports of any kind.

▾ THE FLAMES OF A FIRE SHOW THE MANY DIFFERENT SHADES OF ORANGE.

▸ THIS GINGER KITTEN WILL GROW UP TO BE BRAVE, FRIENDLY AND FULL OF FUN.

Curiosity is one of the driving characteristics of the orange vibration and this brings with it exploration and creativity, particularly on practical physical levels. It tests, then accepts or rejects. It has impetus, self-reliance and practical knowledge.

Orange strength is subtle – it stimulates gently. It broadens life and is very purposeful. Orange breaks down barriers and gives the courage to make changes and face the consequences, good or bad. Because the orange energy is purposeful and has an instinct for moving on, it can creatively remove those blocks that cause restriction and stagnation.

The orange personality is genial, optimistic, tolerant, benign and warm-hearted, believing in friendship and community. The unkind practical joker is negative

▲ Boost a party atmosphere by adding orange decorations to enhance communication between guests.

▶ Orange is the colour of the sacral chakra and governs the gut instincts.

It governs the gut instincts and it enables you to become aware of the needs of your physical body.

orange. A balance of orange energy brings a willingness to get involved; it gives you the ability to fill your time creatively.

## Orange and the body

The lower back, lower intestines, the kidneys, adrenal glands and abdomen are all linked to orange.

▼ In the flower world, orange represents the doctor.

## When orange can help

• Grief, bereavement and loss can all be treated with orange. Orange vibrations will bring you through the shock of deep outrage and will give added strength where it is needed to pull through adversity. • It can also be useful when there is an inability to let go of the past. Orange removes the inhibitions and psychological paralysis that occur when people are afraid of moving forwards in their life. • Orange can help with the fear of enjoying sensual pleasure, it can relieve over-seriousness, a feeling of bleakness and boredom, or a lack of interest in the world outside.
• Orange can be used to treat asthma, bronchitis, epilepsy, mental disorders, rheumatism, torn ligaments, aching and broken bones.

# The energy of yellow

**Yellow is the brightest colour of the spectrum. Its sunny hue brings clarity of thought, warmth and vitality. Yellow pinpoints issues and leaves no stone unturned in its search for understanding.**

THE CHARACTER OF YELLOW

The yellow vibration is concerned with discrimination and decision-making, both skills which are constantly needed for physical and mental well-being. Yellow is the colour of the scientist. It unravels problems and focuses the attention, loves new ideas and is flexible and highly adaptable. Yellow has no hesitation; it decides quickly and acts at once. It smartens the reflexes.

Yellow is the great communicator and a favourite pastime is networking. It has financial

▲ YELLOW REPRESENTS MENTAL VIGOUR AND CAN GIVE YOU ENERGY WHEN YOU NEED IT.

ambition – though holding on to money may be difficult. Yellow has the ability to get things done. It has self-control, style and plenty of sophistication.

▼ YELLOW SWEEPS AWAY CONFUSION AND HELPS YOU THINK CLEARLY.

## SHADES OF YELLOW

As with all colours, different hues of yellow will create markedly different responses. Pale primrose yellow is associated with great spirituality, questioning the world beyond, whereas a clean, clear yellow empties the mind and keeps it alert. Acid yellow can promote feelings of suspicion and negative criticism, and a tendency to bear grudges and resentment.

▲ SURROUNDING YOURSELF WITH YELLOW CAN HELP TO ENHANCE YOUR SENSE OF SELF-ESTEEM AND SELF-WORTH.

Yellow broadcasts a feeling of well-being and self-confidence. People feel good around those under the yellow ray. They are sunny and willing, unless they are upset, when they can be acid and sharp-tongued.

## YELLOW AND THE BODY

The colour yellow is connected to the pancreas, liver, skin, solar plexus, spleen, gall bladder, stomach

◀ YELLOW IS THE COLOUR OF THE SOLAR PLEXUS CHAKRA, AND GOVERNS THE STOMACH.

## WHEN YELLOW CAN HELP

• Use yellow when you need to enliven a sluggish system: it will help to clear away toxins and stimulate the flow of gastric juices so improving nutrient digestion. • It can also be used to treat menopausal flushes, menstrual difficulties and other hormonal problems.
• Yellow is the great eliminator that clears toxins from your system. So apply if you are suffering from frequent minor illnesses, intolerances and allergies or constipation.
• Feelings of lethargy and depression brought on by dull weather respond well to a dose of yellow light, which can also help improve a poor memory or an inability to study. • Yellow can help to improve self-esteem, and reduce negativity and anxiety.
• In cases of diabetes, rheumatism and anorexia nervosa, yellow can sometimes help to relieve the symptoms associated with the illness.

and nervous system. Both the immune system and the digestive system rely on yellow to keep the gastric juices flowing. This colour helps to clear blockages of all kinds.

# The energy of green

**The colour green is found midway in the spectrum. It is made up of two colours: yellow and blue. Yellow brings wisdom and clarity while blue promotes peace. Green's basic qualities are balance and harmony.**

THE CHARACTER OF GREEN

Whereas reds, oranges and yellows are warm, and blues, indigo and violets are cool, green can be either. Green aids the memory, which makes it an important healing colour. Most physical and mental illnesses result from events in the past. Green can release these traumas.

Green is the colour of the plant kingdom. It stands for growth and therefore change, since life is a process of transformation from one

▼ THE GREEN OF FRESH HERBS CAN PROMOTE A SENSE OF HARMONY.

state to another. Growth needs balance and order for it to be sustainable, with each stage acting as a foundation for the next.

Green energy has to do with the pushing back of boundaries, of growing beyond what is known. Because green is connected to the heart it must develop relationships with the things around it, but it also needs a degree of control and power, which may be supportive or destructive. Positive green is the giver: sensible, socially aware, helpful and selfless. Green is about finding self-awareness which helps to bring self-acceptance.

Green is the vibration of relationships, of understanding the needs of others. In a positive, caring relationship, both lives are enriched and expanded and your interaction with the world is broadened. When a relationship is negative or manipulative, your own potential for understanding the world is curtailed and restricted.

The green personality is prosperous and loves to share what it accumulates. Green may have a conflict of ideas but it always strives to maintain the status quo. Green has the ability to discriminate. Used in a positive manner this can promote tolerance.

## GREEN AND THE BODY

The colour green is connected to the shoulders, chest, lower lungs, thymus gland and heart.

▼ PARKS ARE A HAVEN FOR CITY DWELLERS, HELPING THEM APPLY GREEN IN THEIR LIVES.

## WHEN GREEN CAN HELP

• Problems with personal relationships, especially when there is a difficulty with over-dominance or subservience, can be helped by green, as can feelings such as envy, jealousy and greed. The desire to dominate or possess is a negative tendency which green can help.
• Claustrophobia or feelings of restriction caused by being housebound or confined, or feelings of being trapped by other people's rules and regulations can be counter-acted by the green vibration.
• Green can restore stability to any situation. It helps to counteract biliousness and a feeling of nausea.

# The energy of blue

**The colour blue has a stillness about it. It values honour, integrity and sincerity. Blue thinks before acting and proceeds steadily and with caution. It is tranquil and avoids drawing attention to itself.**

THE CHARACTER OF BLUE

There are two aspects of blue. One is the process of communication and the flow of energy, and the other is the experience of rest and peacefulness.

Blue is the spirit of truth and higher intelligence. It is spiritually calming, the colour of the writer, poet, and philosopher. The head and the heart speak directly through the blue throat when there is a need to communicate clearly. Honesty and integrity are key blue qualities, and so if blue is lacking, attempts at self-

▲ GAZE AT THE SEA OR THE SKY FOR A NATURAL DOSE OF BLUE. IT WILL INSTIL A SENSE OF PEACE AND TRANQUILLITY.

expression can lead to frustration and disappointment. However, a blue personality that is out of balance can be subtly (or even unconsciously) manipulative. It dislikes upsets and arguments, but may cause them indirectly.

Blue is a cool vibration; it is the tranquil spirit, the colour of contemplation, and it brings rest. It can help to heal inflammations in the body by cooling the area down, and can also help to counteract infection.

This quality of peace gives blue a sense of detachment from emotional turmoil. It is not overwhelmed by closeness or

▼ DIVING IS THE PERFECT PASTIME FOR PEOPLE WITH AN ON-GOING NEED FOR BLUE.

◀ ON A CLEAR SUNNY DAY, BEING ON WATER WILL FILL YOU WITH BLUE ENERGY.

detail, having the possibility of greater perspectives. The blue personality brings a wisdom to love. Blue is also linked to loyalty. This is the quality that can lead you towards the source of devotion.

The sky blue hue encourages a freedom of spirit. It brings solace where cruelty and brutality have occurred. It is a universal healing colour as it constantly creates – and maintains – calm, while overcoming obstacles with no apparent effort.

### BLUE AND THE BODY

The colour blue is concerned with the throat area, upper lungs and arms, and the base of the skull. It relates to weight gain. The connected glands are the thyroid and parathyroids. Infections in the throat area are often psychologically related to not speaking out. Since the blue personality hates arguments, it may even resort to coughing and spluttering to avoid any form of confrontation.

## WHEN BLUE CAN HELP
• Coughs, sore throats, vocal problems, teething and ear infections can all be treated with blue. A stiff neck, which can represent the fear of moving forwards, also responds. • Blue is particularly useful in reducing the temperature of a fever in adults and children. • Blue can help to calm those who are over-excited or agitated. When used for people with terminal illnesses it can bring a tremendous feeling of peace.

▶ BLUE IS THE COLOUR OF THE THROAT CHAKRA, AND RELATES TO PERSONAL EXPRESSION.

# The energy of indigo

 Indigo has a strong belief in law and order and a great love of tradition. However, it can also be a transformer, a defender of people's rights, and it has an affinity with a deep inner world.

### THE CHARACTER OF INDIGO

The indigo vibration is related to subtle perceptions, such as clairvoyance and other psychic skills. The deep, directionless depths of indigo can heighten our awareness of what is not immediately apparent.

The indigo personality loves structure and hates untidiness. It may ally itself with the Establishment, often upholding the social order in a positive, constructive way. However, a weak indigo personality may become bossy (and over-controlling), or a slave to rigid ideas.

▲ INDIGO PEOPLE WILL OFTEN SEEK SOLITUDE TO DEEPEN THEIR EXPERIENCE OF THE SPIRITUAL OR MYSTICAL REALMS.

When in tune with its inner qualities, the indigo personality can be self-reliant, stepping aside from the world to come up with new ways of thinking. Indigo is an ideal colour for contemplative and spiritual pursuits, such as solitary meditation and visualization, where the inner senses are the most important. Indigo is a stronger philosopher than blue.

The indigo personality may aspire to be a spiritual master, an inspired preacher or writer. Indigo can reconcile science and religion.

◀ GAZE INTO THE INDIGO OF THE MIDNIGHT SKY TO PREPARE FOR THE NEXT STEP IN LIFE.

▶ LIKE A BOLT OF LIGHTNING, INTUITIVE
INDIGO REALIZATIONS OFTEN OCCUR
ALMOST INSTANTANEOUSLY.

It has a pioneering essence, but pioneers with insight. Negative indigo is the believer who has become a fanatic: blind devotion is an indigo failing. Addictions relate to negative indigo.

The flow of indigo energy creates an internal communication that manifests as profound thought processes, new insights, philosophy and intuition. The indigo vibration enhances and heightens awareness, while maintaining integrity. Stillness and contemplation can lead to a "super-cooled" state of indigo, in which intuition and sudden clarity of understanding can occur. The depths of indigo may seem mysterious, but its influence can yield pertinent information.

### INDIGO AND THE BODY

The bone structure, especially the backbone, the pituitary gland, lower brain, eyes and sinuses are all represented by the colour indigo.

◀ THE INDIGO VIBRATION OPENS
UP THE "THIRD EYE".

## WHEN INDIGO CAN HELP

• Indigo is the strongest painkiller in the spectrum and is a great healer. It can be used to combat many illnesses, among them bacterial infections, and the results of air, water and food pollution.

• Indigo can help acute sinus problems (which psychologically are often uncried tears from childhood), chest complaints, bronchitis and asthma, lumbago, sciatica and migraine. Over-active thyroid, growths, tumours and lumps of any kind, diarrhoea and kidney complaints also respond to the use of indigo.

• The sedative influence of indigo can be helpful in lowering high blood pressure.

• Emotional and mental agitation can also be cooled and quietened by the calming effects of indigo. It is the perfect colour to induce a deep, healing peace.

# The energy of purple

 **Purple can achieve great humility, even to the point of sacrificing itself for the benefit of others, without being a victim. It also has the ability to integrate psychic perception into everyday life.**

### THE CHARACTER OF PURPLE

The key to understanding the energy of purple is to see how its component colours, red and blue, work together: red is dynamic, while blue is quietening. Purple brings a new dynamism to blue's still qualities, and stability to the frenetic activity of red. Concepts and ideas are thus better able to find some real application. Purple is associated with imagination and psychic inspiration.

There is a danger that purple can become very arrogant. Where this happens inspiration becomes fanaticism and megalomania and imagination turns into fantasy and

▲ PURPLE IS A GREAT PROTECTOR. IT IS RELIABLE AND SOLID, LIKE A HIGH AND MIGHTY MOUNTAIN RANGE.

delusion. The purple energy, because it seems to extend beyond current knowledge into unknown regions, can trap the spiritual dreamer in a world of unrealistic wishful thinking.

If fantasy about the unknown can be avoided, purple energy can bring enlightenment and healing. It integrates energies at all levels, and as healing requires the building up of new systems (red), according to accurate information (blue), so purple energy can accelerate healing, both physical and emotional.

◄ PURPLE ENERGY COMBINES GENTLENESS WITH POWER.

◄ PURPLE IS THE COLOUR OF THE CROWN CHAKRA, WHICH GOVERNS THE BRAIN.

The skill of integration is aided by purple. As the colour combines opposite energies, so it can help people who also need to work with an array of disparate things. It is often associated with the richness and diversity of ceremony, and with rulers and spiritual masters. Clergymen,

## CAUTION

Purple light should never be directed on to the face, but only to the back of the head. It should be used very sparingly, as long exposures may be depressing. It is not recommended for use with children. The antidote to an overload of purple is exposure to golden light.

musicians and painters all work with the colour purple. Humility is a key aspect, but negative purple can be belligerent and treacherous.

### PURPLE AND THE BODY

The top of the head – the crown, the brain and the scalp – is represented by purple, as is the pineal gland.

◄ LAVENDER IS A GENTLE BUT VERY POWERFUL HEALER.

## WHEN PURPLE CAN HELP

• Purple can be used to treat any kind of internal inflammation, or heart palpitations or headaches. • The immune system and strained nerves can also benefit from the use of purple which enhances the natural healing energy of the body, strengthening the immune system.
• When there is a need to rebalance life, especially if it is lacking in a creative aspect, purple can increase the ability to use the imagination in practical ways and help to integrate new skills into everyday life.
• Purple can calm hyperactive states.

# The energy of black

 **Black is connected to the secret mystery of darkness. It contains every colour within itself, absorbing all light that falls on it and giving out nothing except a promise. It is linked to unseen, hidden and fearful experiences.**

### THE CHARACTER OF BLACK

Black is the energy of gestation and of preparation. It has often been associated with winter and with the promise of seeds lying buried and dormant awaiting spring's growth and the new life to come.

Black is the colour of the person who keeps control by not giving information to others. Someone wearing black continuously may be saying that there is something absent from his or her life. Negative black believes that all is ended, there is nothing to look forward to. It is afraid of what is coming next.

When the energy of black is harnessed in a positive way, it can provide the discipline necessary to work through difficul-

◀ BLACK CLOTHES SUGGEST SELF-DISCIPLINE.

▲ THE COLOUR BLACK IS OFTEN SEEN AS NEGATIVE, BUT IT CAN BE THE PRECURSOR OF CHANGE FOR THE BETTER.

ties and achieve freedom. Working towards the light in any way will involve using the magic of black. Black can complete the incomplete. The mystic arts relate to black.

### BLACK AND THE BODY

There are no parts of the body specifically connected to black except when seen on X-rays or in the aura as disease.

### WHEN BLACK CAN HELP
- Use black in a positive way to encourage self-discipline.
- To break the stagnation of black, a small addition of colour will help the person trapped in black to reach out.

# The energy of white

**White is what is perceived as the entire visible light spectrum, the complete energy of light, and so it stands for wholeness and completion. White is next to the cosmic intelligence of brilliance – but has a denser brilliance.**

### THE CHARACTER OF WHITE

Many cultures associate white with purity and cleanliness, openness and truth. It is often used to denote holiness. It reflects all the light that falls on it, thus radiating all the colours of the rainbow.

White's fundamental characteristic is equality: all colours remain equal in white's domain. It is also a symbol of unity and faith. White has a sense of destiny. Everything is clear and explicit. It also has a cold quality. As a vibration of purification, white can help to clarify all

▾ "PURE AS THE DRIVEN SNOW", A PHRASE THAT LINKS THE TWO ASPECTS OF WHITE.

▲ BURNING PURE WHITE CANDLES WILL BRING A PURITY OF THOUGHT AND OPENNESS TO NEW EXPERIENCES IN YOUR LIFE.

aspects of life, giving the energy to sweep away all physical blocks and ingrained emotional patterns.

### WHITE AND THE BODY

The eyeball is connected to the colour white: its differing shades of whiteness are used in the diagnosis of illness.

### WHEN WHITE CAN HELP
• White has the ability to radiate out all colours, allowing development in any direction, so it is a good choice when you need some impetus.
• Wear white as a tonic to top up the colours in your body's system.

# The energy of gold

**True gold has a belief in honour among men. It has the gift to release and forgive. Gold is related to the wise old sage. It is warm and sparkling, while its light-reflecting quality brings illumination to the mind and body.**

### THE CHARACTER OF GOLD

Gold is purity. It is the soul's experience of all that is past. It has access to knowledge and – most important – to knowledge of the self. Gold means "I am". It does not seek, it has already found. From its deep understanding it is able to forgive and let go of the past. It expands the power of love because it trusts completely and has no vice.

Negative gold's conceit is that of privilege and belief in itself as more worthy than others.

▲ THE GOLDEN LIGHT CAST BY THE SUN TURNS THE LANDSCAPE INTO A RICH AND UPLIFTING COLOUR.

It will blow its own trumpet, but true gold respects and appreciates the value of others.

### GOLD AND THE BODY

No parts of the body connect with gold, an offshoot of yellow, but it can be seen in auras.

▼ GOLDEN BEACH HOLIDAYS CAN CAPTURE THE TRUE, NOBLE SPIRIT OF GOLD.

### WHEN GOLD CAN HELP
• Physical and psychological depressions can be helped by gold as it is uplifting and dissipates negative energy.
• Any kind of digestive irregularity, rheumatism, arthritis, underactive thyroid can all be helped by gold. It will also reduce scars.

# The energy of silver

**Silver has a bright reflective quality which can create illusions and promote fluidity. It brings freedom from emotional restrictions. It is related to the moon and can light up our path.**

THE CHARACTER OF SILVER

Silver is the thread of cosmic intelligence. An invisible silver cord is said to attach humanity to "the other side". It is able to still the emotions and is a great tranquillizer. Silver brings a clarity which helps resolve disputes. It takes an unbiased stand.

Negative silver shows up in relationships in which there is no substance, just delusion. People who fall in love with stars of the silver screen are under this negative influence. Professions that create make-believe also work under silver's influence.

◀ SILVER REPRESENTS ENDURANCE AND IS OFTEN USED TO MAKE TROPHIES.

SILVER AND THE BODY

The feminine dimension of the self is silver, whether it resides in a male or female body. Bathe in the moonlight to restore your equilibrium.

▾ SILVER CUTLERY CAN PROMOTE BALANCED AND FRIENDLY MEALTIME CONVERSATION.

▾ SILVER IS A COLOUR FOR THOSE WHOSE JOBS INVOLVE THE ART OF MAKE-BELIEVE.

## WHEN SILVER CAN HELP
• Silver brings freedom from emotional restriction: it is the great tranquillizer.
• Silver reflects mistakes without distortion. It harmonizes and brings about a fluid state of consciousness.

# The energy of blends

 Turquoise combines the calming, balancing qualities of green and the cool, quiet flow of blue with the warmth of yellow. Pink is also a blend, combining red and white. This mixture promotes consistency of affection.

### THE CHARACTER OF TURQUOISE

In the body, turquoise is related to the throat and chest. The energy of turquoise allows self-expression, as the green quality of growth is added to the blue quality of communication, while the yellow explores information through feelings and emotions. A wonderful healing colour for the central nervous system, turquoise is a colour that allows you to stand still for a while and think only of yourself. The turquoise personality's basic motivation is to seek self-fulfilment in a personal relationship.

## WHEN TURQUOISE CAN HELP
• When the throat and chest need soothing, there is low energy, or a failure to fit in, turquoise can help.

## WHEN PINK CAN HELP
• In any turbulent or aggressive situation, pink can help to calm violent emotions and it will provide energy to move out of a negative situation.

### THE CHARACTER OF PINK

The quality of pink energy depends on how much red is present. White stands for equality, red is the motivation to achieve a goal. Pink represents caring and tenderness and a limited exposure to pink can temper aggressive behaviour. The richer shades can help to improve self-confidence and assertiveness while the paler shades are more protective and supportive.

◀ PLACE THE COLOURED CRYSTAL OR STONE NEAR THE AREA THAT REQUIRES HEALING.

# The energy of neutral colours

**Brown is a colour of the earth and the natural world. It is the colour of solidity, preferring not to take risks. Grey is the true neutral colour, the bridge between white and black, where innocence and ignorance meet.**

### THE CHARACTER OF BROWN

Brown is a colour of practical energy. The brown personality is a deep thinker and can be very single-minded.

Like black, brown represents the seed waiting patiently to develop its full potential. It is the colour of hibernation. It suggests reliability and a state of solidity from which one can grow. Brown can suggest a quiet desire to remain in the background. However, it can also have a dulling effect as it lacks the ability to break out of established patterns. A touch of brown in a room can be warmly comforting.

▲ ▾ THE DARK GREY OF THE MOUNTAIN, ABOVE, GIVES IT A FORBIDDING QUALITY, WHEREAS THE LIGHT GREY OF THE MOUNTAINS, BELOW, HAS AN ETHEREAL FEELING.

### THE CHARACTER OF GREY

When grey contains a high proportion of white it tends to take on the qualities of silver's flow, but darker grey can be draining as the black in it can cause depression. However, grey can also help you to break free from the chains that bind. Negative grey is conventional to the point of narrow-mindedness. When the skin and nails have a grey tint, this can indicate congestion somewhere in the body.

## WHEN BROWN CAN HELP
• Brown is a neutral and non-threatening colour which begets comfort and stability.

## WHEN GREY CAN HELP
• Grey is not commonly used in healing, but light grey is extremely soothing. It can help to restore sanity.

# Hidden colours

**Many colours are actually combinations of other colours. When using colour for healing, it is important to remember that these hidden colours will have a subtle effect that can be beneficial.**

## Colour components

When you are working with colour – particularly when you are using it for healing – it is important to be aware of what are known as hidden colours. For instance, orange is made up of the hidden colours of red and yellow. The eye will see orange but the body will also experience the red and yellow vibrations that are within the orange. Therefore, when working with orange for healing, you should take account of the psychological effects of red and yellow as well as those of orange.

The colour green has its own healing meaning, and also the meaning of the yellow and blue

◀ Orange flowers also radiate the solo energies of red and yellow.

rays that make up green. Turquoise is a combination of all three of these rays. Similarly, purple has red and blue within it, so remember to evaluate these colour effects too. Grey, of course, consists of the hidden colours black and white. Brown is made up of various colours including yellow, red, and even black. Like all colours, brown has a wide range of shades or tints, each with a differing effect in healing. Every shade or tint has a unique combination of hidden colours.

◀ Green's healing quality includes the effects of yellow and blue.

# Complementary colours

**Every colour of the spectrum has an opposite colour that complements it. Knowing these complementary colours will help you to identify which colours you need for healing, support and help.**

OPPOSITES

The complementary colour of red is blue, that of orange is indigo and yellow's is purple. Green, the middle colour of the rainbow, has magenta, which is made up of red and blue.

A knowledge of complementary colours is often useful in everyday life. For example, if you feel extremely irritated by someone's behaviour, you will be reacting to an overload of red vibration within your system. To counteract this, just think of blue, put on some blue clothing or gaze at any blue object. Continue until you feel the anger pass. Or

▸ ALL COLOURS OF THE SPECTRUM HAVE A COMPLEMENTARY COLOUR. GREEN'S IS MAGENTA, AN EXTRA COLOUR MADE UP OF RED AND BLUE.

you may find yourself in a room with yellow decor that you find disturbing. Close your eyes and conjure up the colour purple – the complementary of yellow – to dispel the yellow vibration.

An understanding of complementary colours can be helpful when you are using a lamp with coloured slides for healing. Use a blue slide to relieve the red of irritability, for instance, or a red slide to pull you out of the blues. If you are ever in doubt about a colour, or have a feeling that too much colour has been used, just flood yourself with green light or visualize it. Green acts as a neutralizer, returning balance and order to any situation.

◂ WEARING THE COMPLEMENTARY COLOURS RED AND BLUE CAN HAVE A HAPPY EFFECT.

# Hues, tints and shades

**The description of a colour usually refers to the hue, that is one of the colours of the rainbow. Each colour can vary, it may be light or dark. These variations can be extremely beneficial when used for healing.**

## LIGHT AND DARK HUES

All variations of a hue share its underlying qualities, but their psychological meanings are modified according to whether they are a higher (tint) or lower (shade) tone. Tints are paler (higher) colours which have more white in them. This gives them a stronger healing quality. For example, the white added to red to create pink brings with it a compassionate and spiritual quality. The paler the pink, the greater the healing qualities it

▲ THE RAINBOW CONTAINS THE SEVEN HUES USED IN COLOUR HEALING: RED, ORANGE, YELLOW, GREEN, BLUE, INDIGO AND PURPLE.

possesses. Shades of a colour are darker (lower) and are produced when the basic hue is mixed with black.

In general, the tints are considered positive and the shades negative. But this can be misleading as the darker shades can alert you to problems that you may need to address.

▼ WEARING A PALE TINT OF PINK CAN BRING A STRONG SENSE OF CALM.

### COLOUR DEFINITIONS

Hue: a basic colour in the visible spectrum, a ray

Tint: a hue plus white

Shade: a hue plus black

# Colour categories

**Colours can be grouped into practical categories, based upon the four elements (fire, earth, air and water) and the seasons. These colour groupings relate to personality types, and most people are drawn to one particular group.**

Colour preference

A colour grouping can help in your choice of colours for home decorations, clothes and belongings. You may be drawn to more than one category, which can be useful if you have to compromise with other people over room decor.

Occasionally, your second preference can be useful if you are choosing clothes to create a particular image for a specific purpose, but wearing colours to impress others may feel uncomfortable compared to wearing your natural, instinctive choice.

## Spring – Water

Warm, light tints: turquoise, lilac, peach, coral, scarlet, violet, emerald, sunshine yellow, cream, sand.
Clear, almost delicate colours, that create a joyful and nurturing ambience.

## Summer – Air

Subtle tones, some dark, containing grey: maroon, rose, powder blue, sage green, pale yellow, lavender, plum, oyster, taupe.
Colours that are elegant, cool and contained, never heavy.

## Autumn – Fire

Warm shades (containing some black): mustard, olive green, flame, peacock, burnt orange, teal, burgundy.
Very rich, striking colours that suggest maturity and depth.

## Winter – Earth

Sharp contrasts between hues, tints and shades: black, white, magenta, cyan, purple, lemon, silver, indigo, royal blue, jade.
Bold and powerful colours, with no subtlety.

# Choosing colours

**Your instinctive emotional response to colour can tell you a lot about yourself. It is possible to interpret your colour preferences through their known correspondences to your physical, emotional, mental and even your spiritual state.**

## SIMPLE CHOICE

Given a number of colours to choose from, the process of self-reflection and self-revelation can begin. The simplest approach is to make spontaneous choices. Which colour do you like most, and which colour the least?

The colour you like most will probably be evident in the way you have decorated your home or in your clothes. But it may also be a colour that you need now to help support you in your present situation. Look at the full range of characteristics of that colour for

▲ YOUR CHOICE OF FLOWERS FOR THE GARDEN MAY REVEAL TENDENCIES TOWARDS CERTAIN COLOURS.

clues to other aspects that may help. If the colour you have chosen is an absolute favourite and you have no desire to make other choices, it could indicate that you have become stuck in a habitual pattern.

The colour you like least could suggest an area of your life that requires attention or healing. Bringing that colour energy into your life by adding it to your surroundings may be beneficial.

◀ A CHILD'S CHOICE OF BALLOON MAY GIVE YOU INSIGHT INTO THEIR MENTAL STATE.

## Multiple choice

The process can be developed by making a series of choices. Decide beforehand what question each choice will represent. For example:

**1** What are your physical needs now (activities, food, clothing)?

**2** What are your emotional needs now (peace, fun, company)?

**3** What are your mental needs now (time to study, assertiveness)?

## How to do it

**1** Use the chart overleaf, or collect together ribbons or buttons, at least one of each colour of the rainbow, plus a few other colours.

**2** Lay them out at random on a plain background.

**3** Close your eyes and have in your mind the first question.

**4** Relax, open your eyes and pick up the colour you are immediately and instinctively drawn to.

**5** Repeat the process for each question you ask.

## Interpreting your choices

Look at your colour choice for each question and relate it to the meaning of that colour. You can then introduce the energy of the colour into your everyday life.

▲ A SIMPLE COLLECTION OF DIFFERENT COLOURED FABRICS CAN BE USEFUL FOR DIAGNOSING THE NECESSARY COLOURS.

## Taking it further

You can invent any number of permutations for a series of questions. Here is just one possible list:

**1** Where am I now?

**2** What are my main difficulties?

**3** What is at the root of those difficulties?

**4** What are my priority needs?

**5** What is the best way for me to move forwards?

▼ MAKE COLOUR CHOICES IN YOUR OWN MIND, SIMPLY IMAGINE THEM AND CHOOSE.

# Using a colour-choice chart

**You can use this colour chart to help you with your self-assessment or make your own chart using different paints or pieces of cloth. If you make your own you will be able to include as many colours as you like.**

USING THE CHART

Before you begin to choose your colours, cover the meanings with a sheet of paper. This will help stop your eyes scanning the other page and will prevent the logical and judgemental part of your mind from interfering with your instinctive choice of colour.

Decide how many choices you will make and what each will represent, then close your eyes. For each choice, consider the question you are asking then open your eyes and see which colour you are immediately drawn to.

Record the colour you choose for each question. When you have made all your choices, remove the paper and study the key phrases and questions in the interpretation chart to help you focus your ideas. Where appropriate, introduce more of the colours you have chosen into your life, whether in terms of food, decor or clothing.

COLOUR-CHOICE CHART

DARK RED  RED  ORANGE  GOLD  YELLOW  OLIVE GREEN

GREEN  TURQUOISE  LIGHT BLUE  DARK BLUE  PURPLE  BLACK

WHITE  PINK  MAGENTA  SILVER  BROWN  GREY

# Colour Chart Interpretations

Dark red
You need to keep your feet firmly on the ground. What is taking your attention away from where it needs to be?

Red
You need to take action, now. What is stopping you?

Orange
You need to let go of old emotions and ideas. What are you allowing to block your way?

Gold
You need to relax and enjoy life. What is it that is making you doubt yourself?

Yellow
You need to start thinking clearly. What are you afraid of?

Olive green
You need to reassess where you are going. What hidden factors are stopping your growth?

Green
You need space to gain a fresh perspective. What is it that is restricting you?

Turquoise
You need to express exactly what you feel. What are your strengths?

Light blue
You need to talk to people around you. What do you need to express to others?

Dark blue
You need time to think. What are you so close to that you cannot see clearly what is happening?

Purple
You need to heal yourself. What are you sacrificing to help others?

Black
You need to be quiet and listen. What do you want to hide from?

White
You need to make changes. What do you find painful in the real world?

Pink
You need to look after yourself more. Are you being too self-critical?

Magenta
You need to take time out to heal yourself. Are you risking your own health by overdoing things?

Silver
You need to restore your equilibrium. What are you deluding yourself about?

Brown
You need to focus on practicalities. What areas of your life have you been too dreamy about?

Grey
You need to disappear into the background. What do you want to hide and why?

# COLOUR
# TREATMENTS

Now that you understand how the different colours of the spectrum can influence our moods and attitudes, you are ready to harness their therapeutic properties to rejuvenate the body, make decisions and enrich your life.

Choosing foods based on colour will help you to strike a healthy balance between your various dietary needs, and experimenting with coloured light will enable you to create an effective outlet for your ever-changing emotions. Colour essences and sprays are easy to make from flowers or gel, and are excellent tools for rapid healing. Plus, by incorporating colours into home decoration, dowsing and meditation, you will learn how to become totally at ease in your surroundings.

# Colour and food

**The colour of the foods we eat can have a powerful effect on our physical and emotional state. Eating the appropriate coloured foods can help to rejuvenate and balance the system, making you feel brighter and more alive.**

FRESH FOODS

Wholesome, fresh food is full of colour energy. Seek out foods that are organically grown with no additives, as this will keep the colour vibration alive. Become aware of the colours of the different foods you choose, as your preferences can convey valuable information about yourself.

Your body will normally direct you to the foods that you need to rebalance your health, though habit or advertising may intrude on what should be an important guide for your health. Given a free choice, you will always tend to be drawn to those foods you need, and colour is an important factor.

If you have problems that correspond to certain colours you may wish to increase foods of that colour in your diet. Nutrients such as vitamins and minerals also resonate with particular colours, and these are included in the following lists, as are "non-foods" (foods with little nutritional value) which you may also crave at times when you need instant energy.

▸ RED FOODS PROMOTE TIRELESS ENERGY AND LIVELY ACTION.

## FOOD COLOURS

Red: Gives extra energy, heals lethargy and tiredness
Orange: Creates optimism and change, heals grief and disappointment
Yellow: Encourages laughter, joy and fun, heals depression
Green: Improves physical stamina, heals panic
Blue: Brings peace and relaxation, helps concentration and heals anxiety
Indigo: Puts back structure into life, heals insecurity
Purple: Promotes leadership, heals and calms the emotionally erratic

# Red foods and orange foods

RED FOODS

Foods that are red in colour are generally rich in minerals and are good sources of protein. They increase levels of vitality. Red deficiencies are shown through low energy, anaemia, light-headedness and lack of stamina. Red foods can also help heart problems of an emotional or physical nature. However, professional medical advice should also be sought.

## FOOD FACTS

Fruits: strawberries, raspberries, cherries

Vegetables: red cabbage, beetroot, radishes, peppers (also green, orange and yellow), onions, tomatoes

Other foods: meat, pulses, nuts, fish

Vitamins: B12

Minerals: iron, magnesium, zinc (also orange)

Other nutrients: fatty acids

Non-foods: sugar (also yellow and purple)

ORANGE FOODS

The release of toxins and stress from the body is associated with orange. It also supports the reproductive system and encourages creativity on all levels: orange may help with writer's block. Vitamin C and zinc both resonate with orange and provide an excellent detoxifying combination to help the body rid itself of heavy metals and other pollutants. A lack of orange can cause problems in the area of the orange chakra such as constipation or fertility problems, and also stiffness in the joints.

## FOOD FACTS

Fruits: oranges, peaches, apricots, physalis, kumquats, persimmon

Vegetables: pumpkin, peppers (also green, red and yellow), carrots

Other foods: brown rice, sesame, oats, shellfish

Vitamins: A, C

Minerals: calcium, copper, selenium, zinc (also red)

# Yellow foods and green foods

YELLOW FOODS

The sun is the main source of yellow during daylight hours, but most people work indoors and modern life uses up the yellow vibration dealing with pollution, chemicals, and high stress levels. Yellow foods can help. Lack of yellow leads to exhaustion, tension, restlessness, poor absorption of nutrients, digestive problems, lowered immunity, hot flushes, depression, poor memory and inability to make decisions.

GREEN FOODS

The foods that are of a green nature tend to be very rich in vitamins and minerals, though these can be lost in cooking or storage, so eat lots of fresh fruit and salad. Growing your own vegetables is a great way to ensure their freshness, as well as bringing you in touch with nature. Lack of green vibration creates an inability to relate, a feeling of being trapped, breathing difficulties and negative emotions.

## FOOD FACTS

Fruits: lemon, bananas, grapefruit

Vegetables: grains, peppers, squash

Other foods: eggs, fish, oils, food rich in fatty acids

Vitamins and minerals: A, B complex, D, E, sodium potassium, selenium (also orange), phosphorus, iodine (also blue), chromium, molybdenite, manganese

Non-foods: food additives, alcohol, sugar (also red and purple)

## FOOD FACTS

Fruits: apples, pears, avocado, green grapes, lime, kiwi fruits

Vegetables: cabbage, calabrese, broccoli, kale, sprouts, green beans, peas, leeks, other dark green leafy vegetables

Other: most culinary herbs – marjoram, basil, oregano, parsley

Vitamins and minerals: all vitamins, no minerals

▶ EAT PLENTY OF FRESH GREENS.

# Blue foods and purple foods

BLUE AND PURPLE FOODS

Very few foods are naturally coloured blue or purple, but several work with a blue or purple vibration. Blue foods are useful when the voice and communication skills, glands or organs of the neck need a helping hand. Purple vibration foods can have a remarkable effect on the workings of the mind. Small amounts of basil can help to relax the body while keeping the mind alert.

OTHER WORLDS, OTHER FOODS

Some foods with a purple resonance have long been used in healing. Used carefully, they can open the consciousness to other realms of experience and possibilities. In Central America the peyote cactus (*Lophophora williamsii*) is ritually harvested and used in religious and healing ceremonies, and ayahuasca (*Banesteriopsis caapi*) is collected throughout the Amazon basin for a similar purpose. Both are well known as purifiers of the body and can remove the causes of illness. The herb variety called holy basil is kept by many in the Indian subcontinent as a sacred herb of meditation.

## FOOD FACTS

Fruits: plums, blueberries, black grapes, figs, passion fruit

Blue vibration vegetables: kelp and all seaweed products

Purple vegetables: purple sprouting broccoli, aubergines

Purple vibration plants: St John's wort

Vitamins: E

Blue minerals: iodine
Purple minerals: potassium

Non-foods: food additives and colourings, alcohol, sugar (also red)

◀ BLUE AND PURPLE FOODS OPEN THE MIND TO OTHER WORLDS.

# Healing with coloured light

**The human species has evolved to be reactive to sunlight, so living and working indoors, often under artificial lighting, may be an important factor in undermining health. Coloured light can counteract some of these harmful effects.**

SEASONAL AFFECTIVE DISORDER

Studies of plants have demonstrated that full-spectrum natural sunlight, including ultraviolet (filltered out by most types of glass), plays an important part in maintaining the healthy functioning of plants and animals. The lack of sunlight in winter can be debilitating, and some people suffer from a condition called Seasonal Affective Disorder (SAD), with accompanying mood swings and low energy, when levels of the hormone-like melatonin are reduced in the body. The condition can be treated with several hours daily of bright full-spectrum light.

▲ YOU CAN USE CHROMOTHERAPY ON SPECIFIC AREAS.

CHROMOTHERAPY

On a basic level, chromotherapy, or light treatment, works by using different coloured gels or slides in front of high-powered lamps to bathe either the whole body or specific problem areas. The application of different coloured lights can bring about relief both for the body and spirit. The recipient of the treatment can either lie down or sit in a chair, with the lamp directed towards them. For any serious illness, however, you should always consult a medical practitioner.

◀ USE COLOURED GELS IN FRONT OF A SPOT-LIGHT TO CREATE HEALING COLOURED LIGHT.

### COLOURED LIGHTING

By installing a lighting system that enables you to turn on any colour at will, you can flood the room with your chosen colour. This enables you to be bathed in a colour treatment for maximum health and well-being.

You can achieve the same effect very easily by acquiring a free-standing spotlight and selecting a coloured slide or gel appropriate to your needs. Place the gel over the spotlight, taking care to ensure it is not touching the hot bulb. Turn off any other lights in the room and turn on the spotlight. Sit with the spotlight shining on you and bathe in the coloured light for an instantly available, on-the-spot therapy.

▲ PINK COUNTERACTS AN OVERLOAD OF WHITE, SO PINK FLOWERS ARE COMFORTING WHEN GIVEN TO SOMEONE IN HOSPITAL.

### THE ALL-WHITE ROOM

The perfect healing sanctuary for chromotherapy will be a white room. However, an all-white room in an everyday situation will cause an overload of white; if you are surrounded by it for too long it can cause agitation and frustration. Placing one red object in the room, or arranging flowers of the same hue, will dissipate the sterility that too much white can cause. You can help friends or relatives staying in all-white hospital rooms by taking in appropriately coloured flowers. Blue can help to calm fear and pre-operative nerves, while peach and pink introduce a little stimulation when the patient is recovering.

◄ SATURATE YOURSELF IN THE CALMING BLUE RAY FOR PEACE AND TRANQUILLITY.

# Colour essences

**Colour essences are vibrational remedies. They contain nothing other than water which has been energized by the action of natural sunlight passing through a coloured filter. They are easy to make and effective.**

How colour essences work
Some of the pioneers of colour therapy theorized that the atomic structure of the water was somehow altered and given particular life-enhancing properties. Current medical research is slowly coming to a very similar conclusion and is developing techniques to target specific light frequencies on diseased tissue to restore normal functioning to the cells. Vibrational remedies seem to work by helping the body to return to its natural state of balance after any kind of stress or shock has disturbed it.

▼ Colour essences can be stored for a few weeks in brown glass bottles.

▶ Save scraps of coloured cloth to make colour essences.

Although very simple to make, colour essences can be very effective tools for healing. Rapid release of stress can sometimes feel uncomfortable, and if this is experienced, simply reduce the amount, or stop using the essence for a day or two. Taking essences last thing at night, and then sleeping while they take effect, is a good way to comfortably restore a state of balance. They can also be taken first thing in the morning, which is a good way to make them part of your daily routine, but you may find that you need to take a bit more time getting up, if they affect you strongly.

Like all vibrational remedies, they have the advantage of being self-regulating: the body will only make use of the energy within the essence if it is appropriate.

Colour essences can be used in many ways. A little can be drunk each day in water, or if you place an essence in a dropper bottle, it can be dropped directly on to the tongue. Because they are purely vibrational in nature, the colour essences only need to be within the energy field of the body to begin working, so other methods can also be used. You can spray it around your body for immediate effect; drop a little on to the pulse points at your wrists, on the side of your neck or your forehead; rub it on to the area needing help or the related chakra point; or add a drop or two to bathwater or massage oil.

## HEALING COLOUR ESSENCE

You will need
Plain glass bottle or bowl
Spring water
Coloured gel or other thin coloured material
Brown glass storage bottle
Label
Preservative, such as alcohol, cider vinegar, honey or vegetable glycerine

**1** Fill the bottle or bowl with spring water and cover completely with a coloured gel or cloth. You can also use a sheet of coloured glass laid over a bowl, but the essence will be most effective if only coloured light enters the water.

**2** Leave the bowl or glass in bright natural sunlight for at least two hours.

**3** If you wish to keep the essence for future use, make a 50/50 mix of energized water and preservative, such as alcohol, cider vinegar or vegetable glycerine. It should be kept in a brown bottle away from light. It will keep in this way for many months.

# Flowers and colour

**For thousands of years plants have been used by different cultures to help to keep the body healthy and to fight disease. Many herbs indicate by their colour and shape how they can be used in healing.**

### FLOWER ESSENCES

Paracelsus, the 16th-century Swiss physician and occultist, is believed to have used the dew of flowers for healing and there is some evidence that flower waters were also an integral part of Tibetan medical practices. More recently, in the 20th century, Dr Bach rediscovered the healing properties of flower essences.

Colour flower essences are made by placing flowers in a bowl of water and energizing it with sunlight. As before, use flowers that you are instinctively drawn to.

Red flowers often boost energy levels. The flower essence of scarlet pimpernel (*Anagallis arvensis*), for example, can help to activate energy and clear deep-seated blocks. The elm (*Ulmus procera*) has deep red and purple flowers, and the flower essence helps to clear the mind when fatigue and confusion have set in. In this case, the red stimulates the energy reserves and the purple balances the mind.

Blue flowers will often bring a sense of peace and help with communication and expression. For example, the forget-me-not (*Myosotis arvensis*), as a flower essence, can aid memory and help those who feel cut off from deeper

▼ YOU CAN USE YOUR INTUITION TO CHOOSE PLANTS FOR FLOWER ESSENCES.

▲ THE COLOUR OF LAVENDER VARIES WITH THE SPECIES. USE THE DEEP PURPLE TYPES TO HELP CONNECT WITH YOUR INNER SELF.

levels of experience. Sage (*Salvia officinalis*) has violet-blue flowers that suggest it would be effective in the areas of the head and throat. The flower essence helps to give a broader outlook on life and a balance to the mind, encouraging the exploration of ideas.

Yellow flowers bring optimism and help to release tensions. The flower essence of dandelion (*Taraxacum officinale*) is a muscle relaxant which can also help to release rigid mental belief systems. The way in which the seeds disperse at the slightest breeze can be seen as a symbol of the quality of letting go.

Pink flowers are some of the most powerful healers, and there are many to choose from,

including the pink *(Dianthus)*, the rose (*Rosa damascena*), and the chive flower *(Allium schoenoprasum)*. Pink can help to counteract aggressive behaviour and it also encourages the qualities of generosity and affection.

Since white contains all the colours of the spectrum, white flower essences act generally, giving the body an overall boost. Common elder *(Sambucus nigra)* and chamomile *(Chamaemelum nobile)* are both useful flowers.

Although simple to make, colour flower essences can cause rapid release of stress, which can sometimes feel uncomfortable. If this is experienced, simply stop taking the remedy for a day or two or halve the dose from 6 to 3 drops a day.

▼ YELLOW FLOWERS HAVE ALWAYS BEEN ASSOCIATED WITH OPTIMISM AND CHEER.

# Meditation and visualization

**Colour is a powerful tool in meditation because it has a profound effect on the nervous system, no matter what else may be happening in the mind. Meditating helps you to gather your scattered energies.**

Celestial healing rays

**1** Close your eyes and visualize yourself sitting in a grassy, flower-sprinkled meadow with a cool and crystal clear stream running by you. The day is clear and bright, the sky is blue, with a scattering of soft white clouds and birds are singing in the trees.

**2** Choose a colour that you need for your personal healing and well-being. Next, choose one of the clouds in the sky above you. Let this special cloud become filled with your chosen colour and start to shimmer with its coloured, sparkling light.

**3** Allow the cloud to float over you; as it does, visualize the release of a shower of coloured stars cascading in all directions.

**4** The mist settles on your skin and it gently becomes absorbed through your skin, saturating your system with its healing vibration.

**5** Allow the colour to run through your body and bloodstream for a few minutes, giving your body a therapeutic tonic wash.

**6** Allow the pores of your skin to open so that the coloured vapour can escape, taking any toxins with it. When the vapour runs clear, you can close your pores.

**7** Stay quietly with your cleared, healed body and mind for a few minutes. Take in three slow and deep breaths, before slowly opening your eyes.

◀ Meditate out of doors to receive the calm of green.

# Intuiting colour

**You can use colour as a means of tapping into your intuition and developing your psychic ability. This is a sensitivity everyone has, and you can access it simply by making yourself available and clear of mind.**

### DOWSING WITH CRYSTALS

Use a crystal pendulum. Hold the chain between your first finger and thumb, with the crystal over the palm of your other hand. Direct a question to the stationary pendulum. If it swings round to the right the answer is "yes". Swinging to the left means "no". If it swings backwards and forwards the answer is inconclusive.

You can use crystals of different colours for different questions. For instance, if you are asking about relationships, use turquoise; for business and finance, use green.

▶ HOLD THE PENDULUM AND OPEN YOUR MIND; TRY NOT TO GUESS WHAT THE ANSWER MAY BE.

### USING A COLOUR WHEEL

Draw a circle on white paper and divide it into as many coloured sections as you wish. Hold a pendulum in the centre of the wheel and ask a question. Allow the pendulum to swing towards whichever colour it wants, to give you psychic colour clues. Refer to the profile of your chosen colour to analyse the information.

Remember that any intuitive process can give only indications as to the correct path you need to take. The art is in the interpretation. Monitor your findings – you will be surprised at how many of them materialize.

◀ DOWSING IS A MEANS OF TAPPING INTO YOUR PSYCHIC ABILITY.

# HEALING
# HANDS

Since the earliest times, our hands have been a means of caring, comfort and giving. "Rubbing it better" is our natural response to a child's bumps and bruises and we respond to emotional pain with a hug or caress. Out of this basic instinct, healing traditions all over the world have developed their own unique methodologies, using the power of touch to relieve pain and stimulate the body's self-healing mechanisms.

The following chapter introduces four key hands-on therapies drawn from the East and West: massage, shiatsu, reflexology and reiki. With practice it is easy to include these disciplines in everyday life, using one-to-one contact to help us cope with the pressures of modern living, and to treat minor ailments the drug-free way.

# The power of touch

**We all need to be touched in some way. Touch is a basic human instinct with the power to comfort and reassure on many levels. It can relax the body, calm the mind and encourage healing and emotional well-being.**

### A NATURAL IMPULSE

The desire to touch and be touched is one of our most instinctive needs. The sense of touch is the first to develop in the embryo, and babies thrive on close physical contact with their mothers. The caring, loving touch of another is fundamental to the development of a healthy human being. This need to be touched does not stop with the end of childhood, yet as adults many of us have become afraid to reach out and touch one another. Mistrustful of our natural loving impulse, we have lost touch with

▲ WHEREVER WE FEEL PAIN OR TENSION, IT IS OUR INSTINCT TO TOUCH THE AREA.

ourselves and with the wisdom of the body. The beauty of practising therapeutic touch techniques is that we can begin to re-establish contact with ourselves – and others – in a way that is safe, caring and non-intrusive.

### OUR SKIN

The skin is the body's largest sensory organ. By touching the skin, receptors in the dermis (the skin's second layer) react to the external stimulus and send messages through the nervous system to the

▼ YOUR BABY WILL ENJOY BEING MASSAGED AND STROKED BY YOU.

▲ PETS ENJOY A SOOTHING TOUCH JUST AS MUCH AS WE ENJOY GIVING IT.

▲ IF SOMEONE CLOSE TO US IS UPSET OUR NATURAL INSTINCT IS TO GIVE THEM A HUG.

brain. A gentle stroking technique can trigger the release of endorphins, the body's natural painkillers, and induce feelings of comfort and well-being. More vigorous touching techniques get to work on the underlying muscular structure of the body, stretching tense and uncomfortable muscles and easing stiffness in the joints.

## BENEFITS OF TOUCH

Awareness of the therapeutic value of touch is growing and many touch-therapies are widely used in conventional healthcare to treat pain, ease discomfort and to improve the functional workings of the body. Given the pressures of modern-day living and the increased incidence of stress-related illness, touch therapies also have an important part to play in everyday life. Aching backs and shoulders after a tiring day at work hunched over a computer or stood on your feet, strained leg muscles after excessive exercise, or circulatory problems from a sedentary lifestyle are some of the occupational hazards of adult life. Through the healing power of touch we can learn to take care of ourselves better. Taking the time to channel healing energy or enjoy a soothing foot massage can ease some of the day-to-day tensions of life and put us back in touch with ourselves and our priorities, to feel relaxed and at home in our bodies.

# Massage

**Widely recognized as an effective method of holistic health care, massage is one of the oldest therapies in the world. It is based on manipulating the body's soft tissues with a few simple techniques.**

HISTORY

For thousands of years some form of massage has been used to heal and soothe the sick. In ancient Greek and Roman times, massage was one of the principal methods of pain relief – Julius Caesar allegedly had daily treatments to ease his headaches and neuralgia. In the West, it seems to have

▼ REGULAR MASSAGE HELPS TO MAINTAIN THE COLLAGEN FIBRES, WHICH GIVE SKIN ITS ELASTICITY AND STRENGTH AND KEEP WRINKLES AT BAY.

played a vital role in health care until the Middle Ages, when it fell out of favour with the Catholic Church which regarded such contact as sinful. Its healing powers were rediscovered at the end of the 19th century by Professor Per Henrik Ling, a Swedish gymnast. Ling's methods formed the basis of modern massage – often referred to as Swedish massage. Support for this gentle, non-intrusive treatment has been growing ever since.

### HEALING POWERS

Massage is primarily about touch. When used with skill and care, it can evoke many beneficial changes within the body, mind and spirit. Massage can ease pain and tension from stiff and aching muscles, boost a sluggish circulation, improve the health and appearance of the skin, help the body to eliminate toxins, support the immune system, encourage cellular renewal and aid digestion. As tense muscles relax, stiff joints loosen and nerves are soothed, inducing an all-over feeling of relaxation and well-being. Receiving a massage is a nourishing and calming experience that can increase self-confidence and self-esteem.

### APPLICATIONS

As a therapy, massage can help strains and sprains to heal more rapidly after injury and is generally useful for treating muscle and joint disorders such as arthritis and back pain. However, massage is probably most widely used in the treatment of stress-related disorders. If you are constantly exposed to the adverse effects of stress, it can lead to problems such as anxiety, depression, lethargy, insomnia, frequent tension headaches, hypertension, breathing problems and digestive disorders, to name a few. While not a cure for specific complaints, the nurturing touch of another's hands helps soothe away mental stress and restores emotional equilibrium. There is also evidence to show that a massage treatment reduces the amount of stress hormones produced by the body, which can weaken the immune system. So, having a massage will help prevent as well as cure ill health.

▼ EVERYONE CAN BENEFIT FROM THE NURTURING POWER OF TOUCH.

# Choosing massage oils

**It is usual to work with oils when giving massage. The oil helps the hands to flow and glide over the body and it also lubricates the skin. There are many different types of oil to choose from.**

### VEGETABLE OILS

One of the most versatile massage oils is grapeseed oil. It is light, non-greasy and easily absorbed by the skin. Its neutral and non-allergenic properties make it suitable for many skin types – it may even be used on babies. Soya oil is a useful alternative. Sweet almond oil is also known for its absorbant qualities and non-greasiness – unusual among nut and seed oils, which are generally too rich and sticky to use on their own. However, people with nut allergies should seek advice before applying sweet almond oil.

### ESSENTIAL OILS

Fragrant essential oils have particular therapeutic properties, working on the mind and emotions as well as the physical body. They should never be used neat on the skin, but a few drops may be added to the

▼ MIX 5 DROPS OF ESSENTIAL OIL IN 10ML/ 2 TSP CARRIER OIL FOR A BODY MASSAGE.

### NUT & SEED OILS AND THEIR USES

• Walnut: balances the nervous system; helpful for menstrual problems.
• Sesame: for treating stretch marks.
• Apricot kernel/peachnut/ evening primrose: all promote cellular regeneration; useful for facial massage.
• Hazelnut: for oily skin.
• Jojoba: for oily and sensitive skin; helpful for acne.
• Wheatgerm or avocado: for very dry skin.

▲ A MASSAGE WITH GERANIUM OIL CAN HELP RELIEVE MOODINESS.

vegetable oil base mix (the "carrier"). You may blend up to three oils in any one treatment. Remember that essential oils are highly concentrated medicinal substances and should be handled with care. If in doubt, do not use them, and if any skin irritation occurs, wash the oil off with soap and warm water.

▼ ROSEMARY IS STIMULATING. IT CAN HELP RELIEVE DEPRESSION AND CLEAR THE MIND.

## THE PROPERTIES AND USES OF ESSENTIAL PLANT OILS

- Basil: useful as a massage for regulating the nervous system. It is a good tonic and stimulant, and helpful for muscle cramp.
- Camomile: relaxing; useful for tension headaches, inflamed skin conditions, menstrual problems and insomnia.
- Geranium: refreshing, anti-depressant; useful in blends; good for nervous tension and exhaustion.
- Juniper: uplifting, warming; primary use as a detoxifier, useful for treating cellulite. Avoid in pregnancy and if you suffer from kidney disease.
- Lavender: balancing, refreshing; one of the safest and most versatile of all essential oils; useful for tension headaches, stress and insomnia.
- Orange: refreshing, sedative; a tonic for anxiety and depression; useful for digestive problems.
- Rose: sedating, calming, anti-inflammatory, aphrodisiac; useful for muscular and nervous tension, dry, mature and aging skins.
- Rosemary: stimulating; useful for mental fatigue and debility. Avoid in pregnancy and with epilepsy.

# Preparing for massage

**Giving and receiving massage is a relaxing and enjoyable experience. It is important to work in a supportive environment – one that is warm, quiet and draught-free – and to choose a time when you won't be disturbed.**

## FIRST STEPS

Begin by gathering together all the necessary equipment and materials. This will include massage oils, a selection of clean, soft towels, tissues and perhaps some candles and soft music to set the mood. Make sure the massage area is firm but comfortable; the floor or a futon padded with a thick layer of towels is fine, but an ordinary mattress is generally too soft and springy. It is best to wear comfortable loose-fitting clothes, to take off any jewellery and to make sure your nails are short. Do a few

▲ A MASSAGE IS A RELAXING EXPERIENCE FOR THE RECIPIENT.

stretches and take some deep breaths to calm and centre yourself; giving a massage when you feel tense is counter-productive.

## MAKING CONTACT

The initial contact is a key moment in massage. Gently place one hand on the top of the spine and the other near the base. When using oil, pour it on to your own hands first to warm it, never directly on to your partner's skin as cold oil can cause a shock and undo the relaxing effect. Using smooth, flowing strokes, spread the oil on to the skin then begin the massage.

▼ A WARM ATMOSPHERE AND SOFT LIGHTING CREATE THE RIGHT SETTING FOR MASSAGE.

# Massage strokes

**Massage techniques are relatively simple to learn. They range from a gentle, stroking action that relaxes the body to a more vigorous kneading, pummelling or hacking motion to stimulate and energize the system.**

CIRCLING

This massage movement is useful for moving over large areas of muscle. The action releases areas of tension held in the muscles before deeper, stronger massage is used.

**3** As the left hand continues to circle over the body, cross the right hand over it, dropping it lightly on the skin. Let the right hand form another half-circle before lifting off as the left hand completes its full circle. Repeat several times.

**1** Lay both hands flat and parallel to each other about 10cm/4in apart. Circle both hands clockwise.

**2** Lift up the right hand as it completes the first half-circle. Let the left hand pass underneath.

## EFFLEURAGE

This technique describes long, soothing, stroking movements, using the flat of the hand (or fingers if you are working on small areas). These strokes are used at the beginning and end of the massage. They are also used in between other more stimulating strokes for continuity, and to establish contact with a new area of the body. They have a calming and reassuring effect and should be done slowly and gently.

## PETRISSAGE

Kneading or petrissage movements stimulate the circulation and encourage the drainage of toxins. Generally, a single group of muscles or an individual muscle is worked on at a time. The basic kneading action is similar to kneading dough. Wringing movements also have a similar effect.

**1** Grasp the flesh between fingers and thumb and push it towards the other hand. As you release the first hand, your second hand grasps the flesh and pushes it back towards the first hand. It is a continuous action, alternating the hands to squeeze and release.

## WRINGING

Like petrissage, wringing relies on the action of one hand pushing against the other to create a powerful squeezing action.

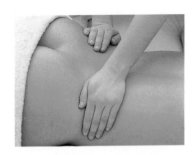

**1** Place your right hand over the hip opposite to you and cup your left hand over the hip closest to you. Slide your hands towards each other with enough pressure to lift and roll the flesh on the sides of the body.

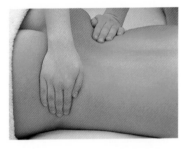

**2** Decrease the pressure as you stroke across the back to your original position, hands passing each other to the opposite sides of the body. Without stopping, immediately begin to slide them back. Stroke your hands back and forth continuously while you wring up and down the lower back area.

### FRICTION

Use friction techniques, such as pressure and knuckling, to work on specific areas of tightness and muscle spasm. Pressure techniques are less painful when performed along the direction of the muscle fibres.

**1** To apply static pressure, press firmly into the muscle with the thumbs. Lean into the movement with the body, slowly deepening the pressure and then release.

**2** To release tension up the sides of the spine, use the knuckles in a loosely clenched fist on either side of the spine to produce rippling, circular movements.

### CAUTION
Do not use tapotement on bony areas of the body. Never apply pressure on or below broken or varicose veins.

### TAPOTEMENT

These movements are fast and stimulating, improving the circulation, and toning the skin and muscles. They are useful for working on fleshy areas of the body. Remember to keep your hands and wrists relaxed.

**1** Cup the hands and make a brisk cupping action against a fleshy area, alternating the hands.

**2** Use the outer edge of the palm and a chopping or hacking motion with alternate hands. Work rhythmically and rapidly.

# Shiatsu

**The word shiatsu means "finger pressure" in Japanese. It is a method of holistic healing that is based on applying pressure to key points on the body. Unlike most other forms of bodywork, you remain fully clothed during treatment.**

HISTORY

Shiatsu was developed in Japan in the early 20th century and has its roots in Traditional Chinese Medicine (TCM). A basic idea in TCM is the concept of the life force, known as "chi" in Chinese and "ki" in Japanese. The life force is the fundamental essence or spirit of life. Invisible like the air that we breathe, it is the energy that animates and nourishes all living things. Ki flows through the human body, circulating through the cells, tissues, muscles and internal organs, and influencing health and well-being on a physical, mental and emotional level.

YIN AND YANG

This energetic life force or ki is recognized as having two polar, yet complementary, opposites called yin and yang.

◄ THE SYMBOL OF YIN YANG REPRESENTS BALANCING OPPOSITES.

Each of these represents different qualities: yin is feminine and passive, yang is masculine and active. The aim of shiatsu is to bring a harmony between the yin and yang energies of the body and its internal organs. This harmony can be disturbed through external trauma such as shock, or injury, or internal trauma such as depression or anxiety. This is when symptoms like aches and pains start to occur and

▼ BACKACHE IS JUST ONE OF MANY COMPLAINTS THAT CAN BE EASED WITH SHIATSU.

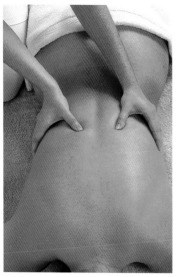

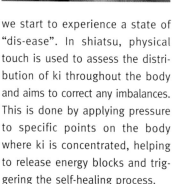

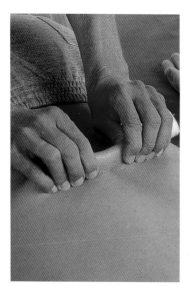

we start to experience a state of "dis-ease". In shiatsu, physical touch is used to assess the distribution of ki throughout the body and aims to correct any imbalances. This is done by applying pressure to specific points on the body where ki is concentrated, helping to release energy blocks and triggering the self-healing process.

▲ ABOVE AND LEFT TOUCH IS THE ESSENCE OF SHIATSU. A SHIATSU TREATMENT CAN CALM THE NERVOUS SYSTEM, STIMULATE THE CIRCULATION AND BOOST THE IMMUNE SYSTEM.

### BENEFITS

Shiatsu is particularly helpful for stress-related conditions, such as insomnia, tension headaches and digestive upsets, where the gentle, caring touch of another can help the body to relax and unwind. It is also useful for improving the circulation and easing out stiffness in the muscles and joints. This makes it useful for treating conditions such as back pain, arthritis or asthma for instance. However, you do not need to be ill to enjoy the benefits of shiatsu. It works very well as a preventive system of health care; it helps to keep the energy flowing freely in the body and has a balancing effect on the body, mind and spirit.

# The meridians

**Vital energy "ki" flows through the body along invisible energy pathways, or meridians. These meridians connect all the different parts of the body together and for good health it is essential that this energy can flow freely along them.**

## BALANCE AND HEALTH

Rather like the veins and arteries of the physical body, the meridians conduct ki, the invisible "blood" of life, to and from the body's cells and organs, bringing nourishment while taking away poisons. If a meridian is blocked, it means that one part of the body is getting too much ki and enters a state of excess, or "jitsu", while another part is getting too little and becomes deficient, or "kyo". The system or organ of the body connected to this meridian is then thrown out of balance and begins to produce symptoms of "dis-ease".

Shiatsu recognizes that any symptoms, however small and insignificant they may appear, are a sign that the energy within the meridian system is out of balance. It is therefore important to deal with minor symptoms, as they may be an early warning of a more serious health condition that could develop if they go unchecked, or may develop into a health problem.

## TSUBO

Along the meridians are highly charged energy points, known as "tsubo" in Japanese, or pressure points in English. By using different shiatsu techniques on these

◀ THE MERIDIANS ARE ENERGY LINES RUNNING THROUGH THE BODY. THEY ARE NOT VISIBLE TO THE EYE AND WILL NOT SHOW UP ON AN X-RAY.

points, such as pressure or stretching for instance, you can help to release any blocked ki and encourage the meridian to "open". This will allow excess ki to disperse or provide a boost where it is stagnant or depleted.

## THE HARA

Ki enters the body through the breath, circulates through the meridians and is stored in the abdomen or "hara", at a special point approximately three finger-widths below the navel. This is the body's centre of gravity and the seat of vital energy. The level of energy in the hara can be used to diagnose and treat problems in all of the meridian lines.

## THE TWELVE ORGANS

There are 12 main meridians, each of which is linked to an "organ" of the body. All the meridians either start or end in the hands or the feet and connect internally to the organ whose condition they reflect.

In shiatsu the organs of the body are perceived in a broader and less literal sense than in conventional thought. In Traditional Chinese Medicine (TCM), the body is seen as a kingdom with each organ having a governing role, an "official" responsible for different functions. When the officials work together and co-operate there is peace and harmony in the land (body). If there is disagreement or disorganization between the different officials, imbalances start to occur.

## LUNG

**Official function:** jurisdiction.

**Responsible for:** the intake of ki from the environment and the total

LUNG
HEART
HEART GOVERNOR
HEART

SMALL INTESTINE
TRIPLE HEATER
LARGE INTESTINE

LIVER
SPLEEN
KIDNEY

elimination of stagnant ki through exhalation.

**Qualities:** openness, positivity.

LARGE INTESTINE

**Official function:** elimination and exchange.

**Responsible for:** supporting the function of the lungs; the elimination of waste products from food, drink and stagnated ki.

**Qualities:** the ability to let go of clutter.

SPLEEN

**Official function:** storage.

**Responsible for:** general digestion of food and liquid; the flow of gastric juices and reproductive hormones; transformation and nourishment of the body.

**Qualities:** self-assurance and self-confidence.

STOMACH

**Official function:** in charge of the body's food store.

**Responsible for:** receiving and processing ingested food and drink; providing information for mental and physical nourishment.

**Qualities:** grounded, focused and reliable personality.

HEART

**Official function:** prime minister.

**Responsible for:** the blood and blood vessels; integrates external stimuli. The heart is the seat of the mind and emotions.

**Qualities:** joy, awareness and communication.

SMALL INTESTINE

**Official function:** treasurer.

**Responsible for:** converting food into energy; the quality of the blood and tissue reflects the condition of the small intestine.

**Qualities:** emotional stability, calm.

HEART
GOVERNOR

HEART

LUNG

LARGE INTESTINE
TRIPLE HEATER
SMALL INTESTINE

LIVER
SPLEEN
KIDNEY

### KIDNEY

**Official function:** energetic worker.

**Responsible for:** providing and storing ki for all other organs; governs reproduction, birth, growth and development; nourishes the spine, the bones and the brain.

**Qualities:** vitality, direction and willpower.

### BLADDER

**Official function:** storage of overflow and fluid secretions.

**Responsible for:** purification and regulation.

**Qualities:** courage and the ability to move forward in life.

▲ TO EFFECTIVELY GIVE A HEALING TREATMENT YOU SHOULD FEEL CENTRED AND COMFORTABLE AND ATTUNED TO THE WORK IN HAND.

### HEART GOVERNOR

**Official function:** joy and pleasure.

**Responsible for:** protecting the heart; is closely related to emotional responses.

**Qualities:** ability to influence relationships with others.

### TRIPLE HEATER

**Official function:** plans construction.

**Responsible for:** transportation of energy, blood and heat to the peripheral parts of the body.

**Qualities:** helpful and emotionally interactive.

### LIVER

**Official function:** planning.

**Responsible for:** storage of blood; ensures free flow of ki throughout the body.

**Qualities:** creative and full of ideas.

### GALL BLADDER

**Official function:** decision making.

**Responsible for:** storing bile produced by the liver and distributing it to the small intestine.

**Qualities:** practical; ability to turn ideas into reality.

# Basic shiatsu techniques

 Shiatsu uses the hands, elbows, knees and feet to apply pressure on specific meridian points. It can also incorporate passive stretching movements to help to loosen the body, manipulate the joints and ease tension.

### FIRM PRESSURE

When giving a shiatsu treatment, focus on your breathing and posture. All movement should emanate from the hara (abdomen); this brings a calm, meditative quality to the mind and will be relayed through your healing touch. When applying pressure, lean on the appropriate point for up to 10 seconds before slowly releasing the pressure.

### THUMB PRESSURE

The bladder meridian is the largest and runs down each side of the spine to the sacrum (the triangular bone forming the back of the pelvis). A steady thumb pressure applied on the sacral points can relieve sciatica and lower-back pain.

### PALM PRESSURE

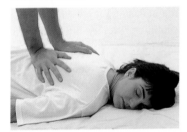

Relax and open out the hands. Shift your weight into the palms and heels of the hands to press firmly but gently along the bladder meridian points.

### STRETCHING

Gentle stretches along the meridians help the body. The practitioner opens the chest by gently stretching the lung meridian in the arm.

## Do-in

This self-massage technique is designed to improve the circulation and flow of ki through the body. It will wake up your brain and aid concentration and mental clarity.

**1** Shake your arms, hands, legs and feet, letting go of tension. Breathe deeply, keeping your back straight.

**2** Make a loose fist with both hands. Keep your wrists relaxed and gently tap the top of your head with your fingers or knuckles. Adjust the pressure as needed and use your fingertips or palms for lighter stimulation. Work your way all around the head, covering the sides, front and back.

### Caution

Seek the advice of a qualified practitioner if you suffer from high blood pressure, varicose veins, osteoporosis, thrombosis, epilepsy, if you are pregnant, or suffer from serious illnesses.

**3** Finish by pulling your fingers through your hair a few times. This stimulates the bladder and gall bladder meridians that run across the top and side of your head.

# Reflexology

**The word "reflex" means to reflect. In reflexology, specific points on the hands or feet reflect another part of the body. By working on these points you can treat health problems elsewhere in the body-mind system.**

HISTORY

Foot and hand treatments have been used in healing traditions across the world for thousands of years, but reflexology in its present form is a relatively recent discovery. In the early 20th century, an American doctor, William Fitzgerald, found that applying pressure to points on the hands or feet could help to relieve pain elsewhere in the body. Eunice Ingham, a physiotherapist, went on to map out these pressure points or reflex

▼ REFLEXOLOGY CAN BE PRACTISED ANYWHERE FOR RELAXATION AND HEALTH.

zones, matching up areas of the body with specific points on the feet and hands. Later, people discovered that these points also relate to certain emotional and psychological states.

BALANCING THE BODY

Reflexology is based on two important principles: that small parts of the body can be used to treat the whole, and that the body has the ability to heal itself. As a result of illness, stress or injury, the body's systems are thrown out of balance and its vital energy path-

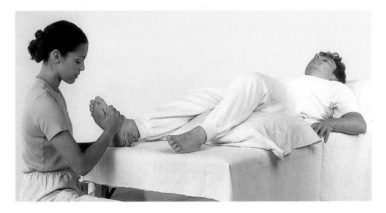

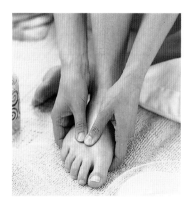

▲ You can practise the healing effects of reflexology on yourself.

ways are blocked. Messages between the brain and nervous system become distorted and the body begins to produce distress signals or symptoms in its call for help. These symptoms of "dis-ease" will show up in various ways (such as headaches or mood swings for instance) and toxic waste matter accumulates around the relevant reflex points. Places on the feet where there are toxic deposits will feel tender, sensitive or painful; or they may feel hard, tight or lumpy, or like little grains. Stimulating these points with massage helps the congestion to disperse and frees up energy blocks elsewhere in the system, encouraging the body to rebalance.

## Treatment

Reflexology is becoming widely recognized as an effective treatment for many health problems. It works well for any condition involving congestion and/or inflammation, such as sinus problems, digestive disturbances, menstrual problems or eczema. It is also an effective method of pain relief and is useful for treating back pain, rheumatism, arthritis or headaches, for instance. A reflexology treatment is relaxing, making it popular for treating stress-related disorders, calming anxiety, alleviating tension and encouraging restful sleep. Many people enjoy reflexology because of its "feel good" factor.

▼ Reflexologists regard the feet as a map of the whole body.

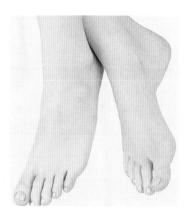

# Reflex zones

**In reflexology the fingers are used to apply pressure-point therapy to certain key points on the feet and/or hands. These points, known as reflex zones, are linked to the body's internal organs and systems and its external structure.**

ENERGY CHANNELS

The body is divided into ten vertical energy zones that run from the head to reflex points on the hands and feet, five on the left, five on the right. These zones are similar to the meridians used in shiatsu. All parts of the body that fall into a particular zone are linked by nerve pathways and mirrored in a corresponding reflex point on the hands or feet.

If there is any imbalance within a zone, the body can produce a range of symptoms that relate to several different body parts that all fall within that zone. Problems with the eyes for instance may indicate an underlying problem with the kidneys. A reflexology treatment, therefore, would not only work on the reflex point related to the eyes, but would also treat the kidneys and any other relevant parts of the body in zone two.

CROSS REFLEXES

Reflexology also works with cross reflexes. Parts of the upper body correspond to parts of the lower body, so that the arms correspond to the legs (the elbows with the knees, the wrists with the ankles), the hips with the shoulders and the hands with the feet. This is useful when an area of the body is too painful to work on directly; for instance, to treat a dislocated right shoulder you can work on the reflex for the right hip.

ZONES ON THE FEET

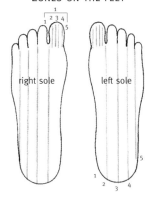

right sole    left sole

◀ LOOKING AT THE SOLES OF THE FEET, THE RIGHT SIDE OF YOUR BODY IS REPRESENTED BY YOUR RIGHT FOOT AND THE LEFT SIDE BY YOUR LEFT FOOT.

## Zones on the body

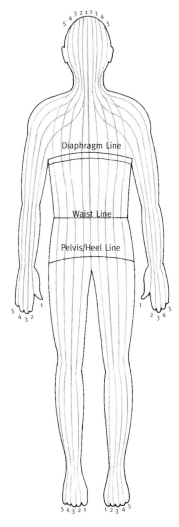

▲ The zones run vertically through the body from head to feet and hands.

## Parts of the body

Both feet together hold the reflexes to the whole body. It can be helpful to divide the body into different areas, tying these in with the relevant zones of the feet. Working from head to foot:

• The head and neck are represented by the toes: the right side of the head with the right big toe, and the left side with the left big toe. The eight little toes represent specific parts of the head, such as eyes, ears, mouth and so on. The kidneys and the eyes are both linked by the energy in zone two.

• The lungs, chest and shoulder areas are represented by the balls of the feet.

• The abdomen is represented by the area from the balls of the feet to the middle of the arch.

• The pelvic area is represented by the soles and sides of the heels and across the top of the ankle.

• The spine is represented by the line that runs along the inner edge of the feet.

• The limbs are represented on the outer edge of the feet, working from the toes to the heels are the arms, shoulders, hips, legs, knees and lower back.

# A mirror of the body

 The feet are believed to mirror the shape of the body, with the organs and body parts appearing in roughly the same position as they occur in the body. Each foot represents the left- and right-hand side of the body.

### Foot charts

When you find a tender or congested part of the foot, you may look for that part on the charts and see approximately which reflex the tenderness lies on. However, picking out certain reflexes in isolation is only really effective in the context of working on the whole foot. Remember also that the charts are only guidelines for interpretation. Every pair of feet will be different and in reality your organs overlap each other, so everything will not "fit" neatly in exactly the same area as shown on the chart.

### The spine

Both feet together hold the reflexes to the whole body. The part that holds the spine therefore runs down the medial line along the inner edge of each foot. The spinal reflex is particularly important. It should always be massaged and the reflex worked thoroughly. The spinal column is not only our main bony support, but it also contains

▲ You can treat your own ailments with reflexology.

the spinal cord, the central energy channel that transmits messages to and from the brain through the central nervous system.

### Pedi-cure

There are more than 70,000 nerve endings on the sole of each foot. By stimulating specific points on the feet, information is transmitted via the nervous system to the brain and a healing process is triggered.

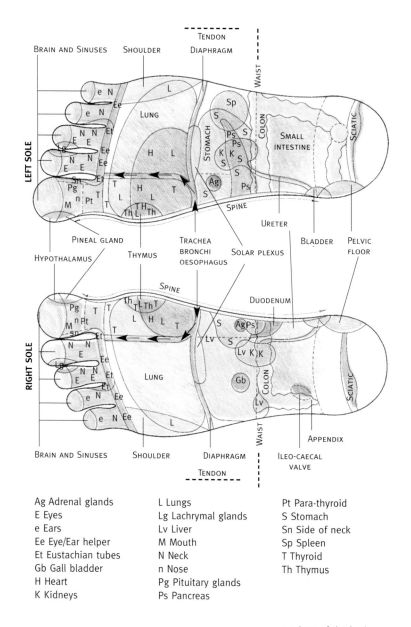

Ag Adrenal glands
E Eyes
e Ears
Ee Eye/Ear helper
Et Eustachian tubes
Gb Gall bladder
H Heart
K Kidneys

L Lungs
Lg Lachrymal glands
Lv Liver
M Mouth
N Neck
n Nose
Pg Pituitary glands
Ps Pancreas

Pt Para-thyroid
S Stomach
Sn Side of neck
Sp Spleen
T Thyroid
Th Thymus

# Basic reflexology techniques

**Applying thumb and/or finger pressure to the reflex points on the feet helps to release congestion and stimulates healing. There are several basic techniques which are simple to learn. The movements should be small and controlled.**

HOLDING AND SUPPORT

When you practise any technique, always make sure that the hand or foot you are working on is secure. It will mean your partner will be more relaxed and you can work much more effectively.

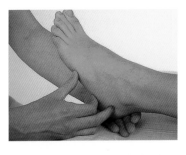

**1** Use one hand to hold the foot and the other to work on it. Position your holding hand near the working hand, not at the other end of the foot as this can feel insecure.

THUMB WALKING

This is the most common method and a useful technique to use all over the foot. It is done with the pad of the thumb that "walks" forward in caterpillar-like movements.

Use one hand only, the other holds and supports the foot or hand you are working on.

**1** Press the thumb of one of your hands down on the skin of the other hand using a firm pressure.

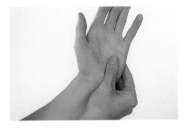

**2** Ease off the pressure and slide or skate forward as you straighten your thumb in a caterpillar movement. Stop and press again. Keep your movements slow, continuous and rhythmic.

### FINGER WALKING

This technique uses the fingers and is useful for bony areas.

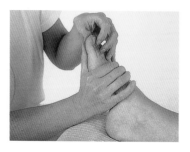

**1** Hold the foot or hand with your right hand and fingerwalk from the tip of the big toe with your left index finger.

**2** Firmly hold the foot or hand with one hand and fingerwalk down the top of the foot towards the toes, using the three middle fingers of the other hand together. This area can be very sensitive so take care not to press too hard with the fingers. Try to keep the pressure firm and even, but comfortable.

### ROTATING

This technique is good for tender reflexes, or for when you want to work on a specific small point. Vary the pressure as is comfortable.

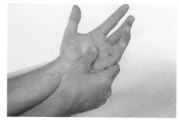

Using a firm pressure, press and rotate the thumb into the point.

### PINPOINTING

Use this technique for deep or less accessible reflexes. Restrict it to the fleshy, padded parts of the feet as it can be quite painful.

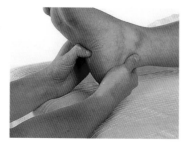

Supporting the heel, press deeply into the tissues with the inner corner of your thumb.

# Top and sides of foot

It is not only the soles of the feet that relate to other areas of the body. These diagrams show the areas covered by the tops and sides of the feet. The whole body may be treated on the spinal reflex through the central nervous system.

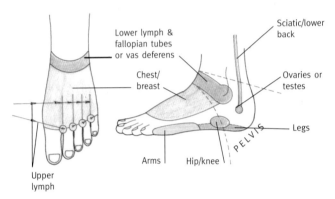

Lower lymph & fallopian tubes or vas deferens

Chest/breast

Upper lymph

Arms

Hip/knee

Sciatic/lower back

Ovaries or testes

PELVIS

Legs

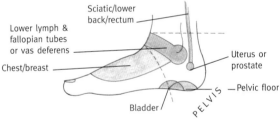

Sciatic/lower back/rectum

Lower lymph & fallopian tubes or vas deferens

Chest/breast

Bladder

PELVIS

Uterus or prostate

Pelvic floor

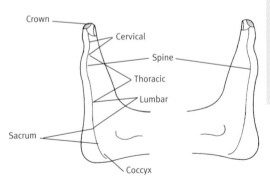

Crown

Cervical

Spine

Thoracic

Lumbar

Sacrum

Coccyx

## THE SPINE

The spinal reflex should always be massaged, and worked thoroughly.

# Hand charts

The hands reflect all the body, as do the feet. Once you have adjusted to the basic layout, the location of reflexes is quite straightforward. Use the hand reflexes when you cannot work the feet for any reason.

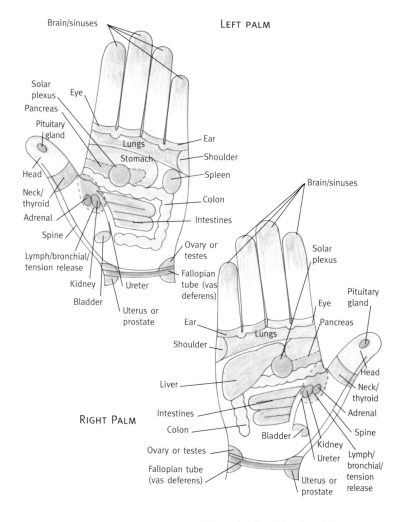

LEFT PALM

Brain/sinuses
Solar plexus
Eye
Pancreas
Pituitary gland
Lungs
Ear
Stomach
Shoulder
Head
Spleen
Neck/thyroid
Colon
Adrenal
Intestines
Spine
Ovary or testes
Lymph/bronchial/ tension release
Fallopian tube (vas deferens)
Kidney
Ureter
Bladder
Uterus or prostate

RIGHT PALM

Brain/sinuses
Solar plexus
Pituitary gland
Eye
Pancreas
Ear
Lungs
Head
Shoulder
Neck/thyroid
Liver
Adrenal
Intestines
Spine
Colon
Bladder
Ovary or testes
Kidney
Fallopian tube (vas deferens)
Ureter
Lymph/bronchial/ tension release
Uterus or prostate

# Reiki

**Channelling divine or cosmic healing energy through the hands is one of the oldest and most profound methods of healing known. Reiki is a special technique that brings the ability to heal within the grasp of everyone.**

## History

Reiki (pronounced ray-key) means universal ("rei") life force ("ki") in Japanese. With its roots in Tibetan Buddhism, the ancient healing methods of reiki were rediscovered in the 19th century by Dr Mikao Usui, a Japanese mystic, during a vision. These methods were regarded as sacred knowledge, and the secrets were passed down from master to student in special initiation ceremonies. Today the tradition of master and student continues, and reiki practitioners have been through special "attunements" with a modern-day master to receive this ancient knowledge and open up a healing channel. It is relatively easy to find a reiki master and become a reiki initiate, but it is possible for anyone to channel healing reiki energy by understanding and applying a few basic principles.

▼ A REIKI PRACTITIONER CHANNELS HEALING ENERGY THROUGH THEIR HANDS.

## Universal law

Reiki is about tuning in to the laws of the universe and working in harmony with them. The universe is a place of boundless energy that flows through space and time, and through everything here on Earth. We are not separate, isolated identities but connected to the universe and everything in it by this cosmic energy, the breath of life that nurtures and sustains us. This energy is sometimes known as the life force and its healing power is love. It is a force for good in the world that transcends time and place, colour and creed, and any negative, destructive impulses that threaten the health and well-being of life. Reiki invites us to open up and trust in this great love, allowing it to flow through us, bringing positive healing wherever it is needed. We can channel this healing energy for the benefit of ourselves and other people, as well as to treat plants, animals and even places.

▲ WE CAN ALL BENEFIT FROM REIKI AND EACH OF US CAN CHANNEL REIKI ENERGY.

▼ REIKI CHANNELS THE ESSENTIAL ENERGY OF THE UNIVERSE TO CREATE WELL-BEING.

## BENEFITS

Giving and receiving reiki is a relaxing experience. It is particularly effective for calming and soothing negative emotional states, for relieving pain and for treating stress-related conditions, such as insomnia, fatigue or tension headaches, for instance. A reiki treatment helps to rebalance the body's energy systems and generally promotes good health and well-being. Done regularly it can help to protect the body against illness and negative influences as it helps to realign the human energy system with the healing vibrations of love and light.

# Reiki hand positions

**In a reiki treatment, the hands are positioned at various places on the body. In order for the energy flow to be focused, the fingers and thumbs are held together, and the hands kept flat or very slightly cupped.**

If you have not been officially attuned to reiki, prepare yourself at a quiet time, when your attention can be fully attuned to yourself. Visualize a stream of golden healing light entering your body through the crown chakra. See yourself as an open and receptive channel for this energy, allowing it to enter and pass through your body via the hands, on to the body of your partner.

**1** Place the hands over the eyes. This position aids clear vision and energizes the eyes.

**2** Slide the hands sideways on to the temples. This position helps to dispel tension in the face.

**3** Bring your hands round to underneath your partner's head, just above the neck so that you are cradling it. This position balances the energy in both sides of the brain and releases mental tension.

**4** Remove your hands and place them with the heels of the palms on the side of the neck and with the palms and fingers lightly on the throat. This can help to release emotional trauma and upset.

**5** Slide the hands on to the top of the chest. This position is relaxing and reassuring. Move to one side and continue down the trunk, placing your hands in a straight line across the chakra points.

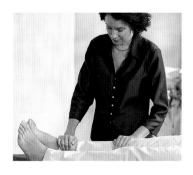

**6** Continue working down, first one leg and then the other in as many stages as feels right. Working along the legs and channelling healing energy helps to balance and relax the recipient's lower body.

**7** To finish, stand at the foot of your partner and finish by placing the hands on the feet, first the upper feet, then the soles. This helps to "ground" the energy so that your partner doesn't feel too floaty or light-headed at the end of the treatment.

# Self-treatment with reiki

**It is a good idea to practise reiki on yourself. This will increase your self-confidence when giving treatments to other people, as you will have experienced its healing powers first hand. It will also nourish and refresh you.**

### REIKI SELF-TREATMENT

You can give reiki to yourself at any time of the day. Some people like to start with it first thing in the morning in preparation for the day ahead. Others find it helpful to end the day with reiki, helping the body to relax and unwind in preparation for sleep. Ideally, it is best to set aside a full hour for a reiki self-treatment, but if this is not possible, 10–15 minutes set aside on a regular basis will bring good results and a healthier outlook.

Either sit in a comfortable upright position or lie down where you won't be disturbed. Set your alarm clock if you have appointments, and unplug the telephone. Close your eyes and centre yourself by breathing gently into the abdomen. Take in a deep breath, hold for a few moments and exhale. Repeat this a few times.

Imagine that golden, healing reiki energy is flowing into your body, circulating along the subtle energy pathways, nourishing every

▲ A REIKI SELF-TREATMENT WILL LEAVE YOU FEELING REFRESHED AND READY FOR THE DAY.

cell and organ. Place your hands on any areas of your body that you feel need particular attention. Leave them there for as long as is comfortable. You may notice that the area of your body becomes warm as the energy circulates.

▲ The flowers, shrubs, even bulbs in your garden will benefit from reiki.

▲ Pets can benefit from reiki too – use it to maintain general health.

## Reiki Anywhere

Remember that there is nothing for your brain to "learn" with reiki. It is a question of being open to its healing powers and willing to let the energy flow through you. Cultivate the reiki habit and bring reiki treatments into other activities. Try relaxing back in a warm bath, and practise the hand positions on your face and torso. Reiki can be worked into a foot massage or a beauty treatment, or if you have a busy day, give yourself reiki as you go along. This can be done while watching television, queuing at the supermarket checkout or sitting in a traffic jam, for instance. Just put your palms anywhere on your body, imagine the healing energy entering you and say to yourself, "Reiki flow!" You will soon feel the benefits.

▼ Greeting the day with a salute to the sun: adding an element of ritual to your morning routine will create a happy day.

self-treatment with reiki **211**

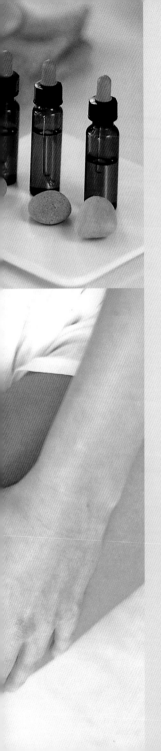

# THE HEALING
# TOUCH

Many common health problems are related to
stress and lifestyle. When we feel overwhelmed
and unable to cope, the body's fine-tuning is
knocked off balance and things start to go awry.
The body produces a range of annoying and
unpleasant symptoms. Many of these minor
ailments respond well to the healing touch of
massage, reflexology, reiki or shiatsu.

The following section includes step-by-
step sequences and useful tips on treating a
range of minor complaints. Some of these
moves can be practised on yourself, while
others require a partner. Follow steps to
improve the circulation and digestion, to relieve
stress, tension, fluid retention, aches and pains,
and to enhance the quality of sleep.

# Start the day sequence

**To make the most of your potential, your bodily systems need to be functioning well as you start the day and to continue to do so throughout the day. The systems and senses can be stimulated with the following sequences.**

INVIGORATING THE BODY

This sequence stimulates all your bodily systems, enabling you to make the most of your potential and start the day in the best way.

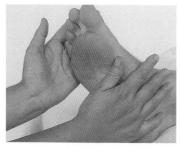

**1** Massage the feet to establish good breathing and the instep to stimulate the nervous system.

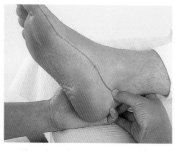

**2** Thumbwalk the spine. Rotate the ankles and toes to stimulate circulation and free the nerves.

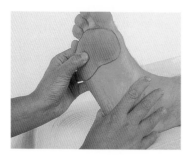

**3** Work the diaphragm, and then across the chest to establish deep breathing to strengthen the body.

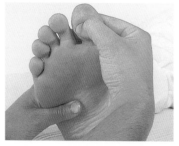

**4** Work the pituitary reflex on the big toe in the centre of the toe-print: this is the master gland.

By working the diaphragm, solar plexus and liver you are enhancing good breathing, which improves planning and decision-making.

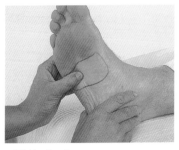

**1** Work the liver.

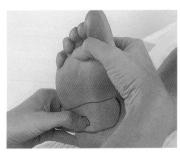

**2** Work the gall bladder.

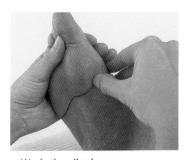

**3** Work the diaphragm.

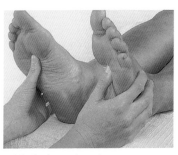

**4** Work the solar plexus.

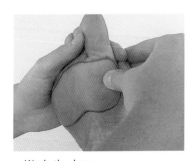

**5** Work the lungs.

### HELPING HANDS

To aid decisiveness, locate the gall bladder reflex on your right hand and rotate on it with your thumb.

# Energy boosters

**If energy is flowing freely around your body you will feel well and find it easier to stay positive. Think positively: the power of thought influences physical health and, conversely, your moods are affected by hormonal balance.**

ENHANCING ENERGY LEVELS

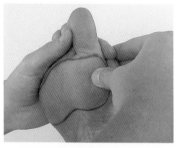

**1** Work the lungs to improve your breathing patterns.

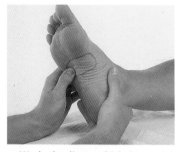

**2** Work the liver, which is crucial to your general health.

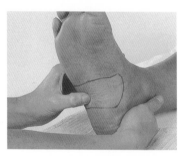

**3** Work the small intestine to aid the uptake of nutrients.

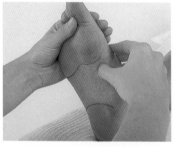

**4** Work the whole digestive area. What you eat is turned into your energy during digestion.

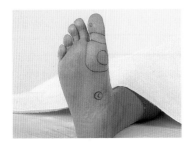

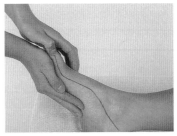

**5** Work the glands on the big toe. Rotate the adrenals.

**6** Work up and down the spine, your central column of energy flow.

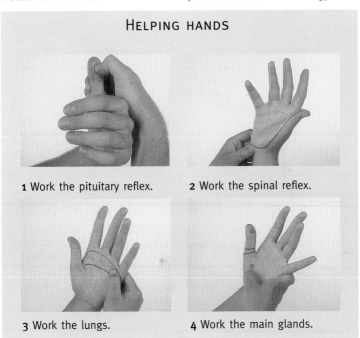

## HELPING HANDS

**1** Work the pituitary reflex.

**2** Work the spinal reflex.

**3** Work the lungs.

**4** Work the main glands.

# Improving skin, hair and nails

To keep your skin, hair and nails in good condition you need hormone balance, good nutrition and effective removal of toxins through the excretory system. Stimulation of the circulation will aid the removal of toxins and the supply of nutrients through the bloodstream.

STIMULATING CIRCULATION

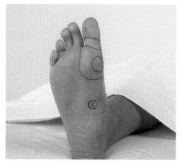

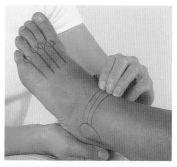

1 Work all the glands on both feet. Your skin, hair and nails are kept in good health by chemicals in your hormones, which are controlled by your glands.

2 In addition, make sure that you give attention to the lymph system on both feet to help remove toxins from the body.

## HELPING HANDS

Work all the glands on both of your hands using the chart on page 205 for reference.

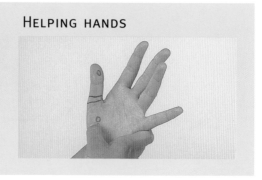

# Enhancing immunity

 Where the immune system is strong, the body will deal naturally with threatening infections so that they cannot become established. Within the context of a full reflexology routine, pay particular attention to the liver, spleen and lymph systems.

IMMUNE BOOSTERS

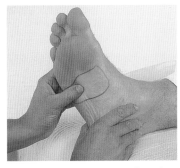

**1** Work the liver to strengthen the whole body.

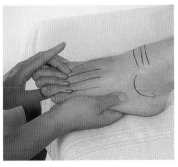

**2** Work the lymph systems on both feet to aid the removal of toxins.

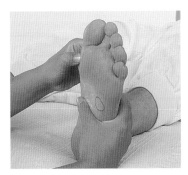

**3** Work the spleen (marked on the left foot) and rotate the thymus gland (for both feet) positioned on the ball of the foot.

## HELPING HANDS

Work the liver and spleen to strengthen your body, and the thymus gland and lymph system to fight off imminent infection. See the hand chart on page 205 for reference as to how the specific areas of the hand relate to these parts of the body.

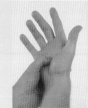

# Easing colds, sore throats and sinuses

 Colds, sore throats and sinus problems all affect the respiratory system. To stimulate them to clear themselves of toxins and encourage uptake of nutrients, you need to work all the toes and chest area.

COLDS

**1** Work the entire chest area to encourage clear breathing. See the charts on page 201.

**2** Beginning with the big toe, work the tops of all the toes to clear the sinuses. Then pinpoint the pituitary gland in the centre of the prints of both big toes to stimulate the endocrine system.

**3** Work the upper lymph system to stimulate the immune system. See the charts on page 204.

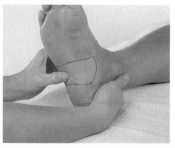

**4** Work the small intestines to aid elimination of toxins and uptake of nutrients. Then work the colon to aid elimination. See the chart.

## Sore throats

**1** Work the upper lymph system, then the throat, and the thymus gland for the immune system.

**2** Work the trachea and the larynx so as to stimulate them both to clear and heal.

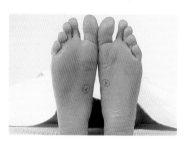

**3** Rotate the adrenal reflex in the direction of the arrow.

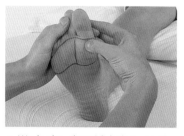

**4** Work the thyroid helper in the chest section, then the whole chest area for the respiratory system.

## Sinuses

**1** Work the sinus reflexes.

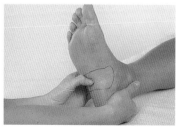

**2** Work the ileo-caecal valve.

# Backaches

**More working days are lost through backache than from any other cause. Common causes of backache include poor posture, injury through straining and lifting, pregnancy, stress and muscular tension.**

Back pain can vary from a dull, persistent, nagging ache to a sharp, searing pain. Tightness in the muscles around the spinal cord constricts the body's main energy pathway, affecting the central nervous system. The pain itself is also very draining. The soothing touch of another's hands can be very healing; reflexology and reiki are both helpful.

REFLEXOLOGY RELIEVER
A simple but effective reflexology treatment can help to release tension and relax the supporting muscles. The inside edge of the foot represents the spine.

1 Thumbwalk along the spine, supporting the outer edge of the foot.

2 Fingerwalk across the spinal reflex, right down the instep, in stripes.

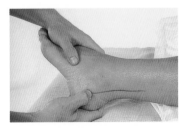

3 Thumbwalk up the helper reflexes.

## TIPS FOR AVOIDING BACK PAIN
• Improve your posture; don't slump but sit straight, make sure your chair supports you.
• Take regular, gentle exercise, such as swimming or yoga.
• Invest in a firm mattress.
• Bend from the hips and knees when lifting heavy objects.

A gentle reiki treatment is another way of helping the body to relax. It can also address the underlying emotional and mental state that may be contributing to the problem. For instance, backache is often caused by worrying and feeling burdened. Lower back pain is linked to problems in the first chakra, indicating insecurity in material matters – such as worry about money.

Your partner should be sitting upright on a backless chair, or lying face down on the floor.

**1** Place your hands in the shape of a T-cross between the shoulder blades and down the spine. This position treats the upper back and shoulder areas, stimulating the heart chakra and surrounding organs. Concentrate on the healing energy of your touch.

**2** Allow your hands to be drawn to any other areas of the back where healing is needed. Finish by placing your hands at the top and bottom of the spine in the "spirit level" position, to balance the energy along the backbone and through the chakras.

# Headaches

**The majority of "everyday" headaches are caused by stress and tension. Other common triggers include eyestrain, hangovers, lack of sleep and exercise, caffeine overload, missed meals and hormonal swings.**

REFLEXOLOGY FOR HEADACHES

A foot treatment can work wonders on a tension headache. Headaches generally mean there is too much energy in the head and eyes, caused by excessive worry, mental work or eyestrain for instance. Reflexology can help to release the energy, encouraging it to disperse through the rest of the body.

**1** For pain relief, work the hypothalamus reflex. This controls the release of endorphins.

**2** Work down the spine to take pressure away from the head. This will draw energy down the body.

**3** Work the cervical spine on the big toe. Work the neck of all the toes to relieve tension.

**4** When we are tense our breathing is tight and shallow. Work the diaphragm area to encourage the breathing to become deeper.

## SHIATSU

This simple shiatsu technique can help to prevent and relieve headaches. It is a movement that many of us do instinctively when we have a headache.

Sit in a relaxed position and gently massage your temples, using small circular movements. Remember to keep your elbows dropped down.

### REIKI HEADACHE SOOTHER

A reiki treatment can help to melt away tensions and restore peace and equilibrium. It is best if your partner sits upright for this treatment, although it can also be done with him or her lying down.

**1** Place your hands on each side of the head at the back cupping the skull. This helps to dispel tension rising from the neck and balances energy in the brain.

**3** Finish by gently placing one hand across the brow, covering the eyes. Place the other hand on top of the head, touching the first hand. Hold the position firmly. This position helps relieve emotional stress and is soothing for the recipient.

**2** Place one hand on the forehead and the other at the base of the skull, cradling the head firmly in your hand.

# Pain relievers

**Muscles are the body's connecting tissue; their elasticity enables us to move. Pain in the muscles may result from injury or from overuse. Cramps are painful, involuntary muscle spasms.**

MUSCLE AND BACK PAIN

Reflexology can help to reduce inflammation and pain in the muscles and joints. It can also relax muscle spasm. Before focusing on the specific area of pain, work the hypothalamus reflex first to help with pain relief.

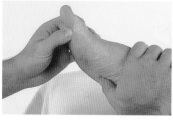

Before trying out the following sequences, gently rotate the hypothalmus reflex. This will help to release endorphins which will make for faster pain relief.

**1** Work the adrenal gland reflexes on both feet. These glands deal with inflammation and aid good muscle tone when they are working effectively.

**1** To relieve back pain, work along the spine to locate the tender areas and disperse some of the congestion.

**2** For lower back trouble, work the helper area by applying gentle pressure and rotating with the thumb.

### Massage for calf cramp

Calf cramp can be triggered by exercise, repetitive action or sitting awkwardly. Cramp may indicate poor circulation or a deficiency of calcium or salt. Massage improves the circulation and alleviates pain. It also helps eliminate lactic acid, a waste product stored in the muscle tissue after exercise.

**1** Apply thumb pressure into the cramped muscle for 8–10 seconds.

**2** Work from the ankle to the thigh using long effleurage strokes.

### Hamstring cramp massage

It is usually underused or ill-prepared muscles that go into cramp during exercise.

**1** Raise the ankle on a small pillow and begin by massaging the back of the thigh using alternate hands in slow, rhythmical stroking movements. Then apply static pressure to the middle of the thigh with the thumbs, holding for 8–10 seconds.

**2** Firmly knead the calf muscle. Squeeze, press and release the muscle using one hand after the other. Finish the massage by doing some soothing effleurage strokes up from ankle to thigh and back down again.

# Tennis elbow and repetitive strain

 Overuse of any part of the body puts a strain on the muscles and tendons and can result in painful conditions, such as tennis elbow or repetitive strain injury (RSI). Both of these conditions can be helped with touch therapies.

TENNIS ELBOW MASSAGE
Inflammation of the tendon running along the forearm to the elbow creates pain. Sportspeople and gardeners are particularly at risk. Massage can help to ease the pain.

**1** Support your partner's wrist in one hand and use soothing strokes along both sides of the arm from the wrist to the elbow and back again. Repeat several times.

**2** Rest the hand against your side. Work up the arm, from wrist to elbow and back, making small circular movements.

**3** Stand to one side of your partner, secure their hand in yours and support their elbow with your other hand. Flex the elbow forward.

**4** Bring the hand back to give the tendons that are attached to the bones a good stretch.

REFLEXOLOGY FOR REPETITIVE STRAIN

Repetitive strain can affect any part of the body that is overused. It is an occupational hazard for keyboard operators, where a stiff neck and shoulders, aching wrists and pain and weakness in the forearm are increasingly common problems. Reflexology can help to ease some of the discomfort.

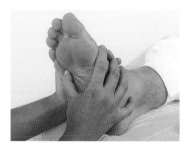

**1** Work the shoulder reflexes thoroughly by using the thumbwalking technique. Gently fingerwalk across the same area on the top of the foot, with the three middle fingers held together.

**2** Rotate the ankles to ease aching wrists and stimulate healing within the joints. Work down the outside of the foot to relax the shoulders and arms.

### TIPS FOR KEYBOARD WORKERS

- Make sure your wrist is well supported. Mouse mats are available with inbuilt wrist supports.
- Take regular breaks away from the keyboard.
- Flex and rotate the fingers and wrists, to keep them supple and stop them from aching.
- Massage hands and forearms on a regular basis.

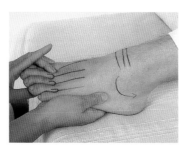

**3** Work the lymph system on both feet to encourage toxins to drain away. Fingerwalk down the lines from the toes towards the ankle, then work around the ankle.

# Fluid retention

**A heavy feeling in the legs and puffy, swollen ankles are typical signs of fluid retention. The problem is often aggravated by hot weather, prolonged periods of standing, premenstrual tension, long haul flights and pregnancy.**

MASSAGE TO IMPROVE CIRCULATION
Excess fluid indicates that the kidneys and/or circulation are not working properly. Massaging the legs and the thighs will improve the local circulation and so bring more blood and oxygen to the muscles. Firm effleurage movements are particularly helpful. They should always be done in one direction, towards the heart.

## TIPS TO AVOID FLUID RETENTION
• Drink plenty of water to help the kidneys flush out (at least six glasses a day).
• Remember to increase your water intake in hot weather.
• Include raw food in your diet.
• Regular massage will improve the circulation and drainage of toxins.
• Avoid prolonged sitting or standing in one spot.

**1** Place your hands on your partner's thigh and stroke upwards to the buttock several times using smooth effleurage strokes. Keep the pressure light but steady, letting one hand follow the other.

**2** Move your hands down to the calf and stroke up to the back of the knee a few times. Repeat these two steps, always starting the massage on the upper leg and always stroking towards the heart.

### SHIATSU MENSTRUAL TREATMENT

Used on the feet, shiatsu can help to stimulate the body's energy system, improving circulation and the drainage of toxins. There are also specific points that can help with menstrual problems.

**1** With a loose fist, tap the sole of the foot. Then gently massage the whole foot thoroughly with both hands.

**2** Massage the web between each toe and then massage the toe joints. The point between the big toe and the second toe is good for period pains (do not use this massage during pregnancy).

**3** Come to the sole of your foot and apply pressure to it with your thumb. This will have a revitalizing effect upon your body and stimulate energy flow.

**4** Use your thumbs to massage the area under the ankle bone. This is a good point to use for any menstrual disorders. Use your thumb and press firmly.

▸ INSTEAD OF SUFFERING FROM PERIOD PAINS, TRY A SHIATSU SELF-TREATMENT.

### USEFUL AROMATIC OILS

• Pine: reducing puffiness in the legs, particularly after prolonged standing and in late pregnancy.
• Geranium, juniper, rosemary: premenstrual fluid retention.
• Fennel, juniper, lemon: detoxifying oils.
• Cypress, geranium, pine: after long-haul flights.

# Improving circulation

**The circulatory system connects all the systems of the body. Its tone and vitality is fundamental to life and to the integration of the whole body. There are many steps we can take to help it function effectively.**

HAND AND FOOT MASSAGE

Cold feet and hands are a sign of poor circulation. When we breathe in, oxygen from the air is absorbed into the blood and carried to the heart. It travels around the body, carrying vital nutrients to every cell and returning waste products for disposal. Poor circulation means that the body's tissues and organs are inadequately nourished and that toxins are not removed properly, leading to many other health problems. A massage will help to warm hands and feet, and improve the circulation.

**1** Using a little oil, massage the palm of the hand with a steady, circular movement of the thumb.

**2** Squeeze down each finger to stretch and loosen the joints, pushing towards the palm. Repeat.

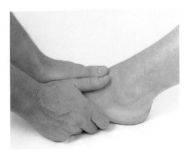

◀ **3** To stretch the foot, use both hands with the thumbs on top and fingers underneath the foot. Keep a loose but firm grip. Move the thumbs outward, as if breaking a piece of bread. Repeat several times, keeping the fingers still while moving your thumbs.

Working a shiatsu treatment on each side of the spine is invigorating and relaxing. Rubbing and rolling techniques are useful for improving the circulation – of both blood and energy – throughout the whole body.

**1** Use the palms to apply gentle but firm pressure down each side of the spine.

**2** Using the side of your hands, vigorously rub down each side of the spine a few times.

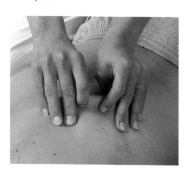

**3** Pinch and take hold of the skin on the lower part of the spine. Lift the tissue and gradually roll it up the spine. Roll the skin from the spine, out towards the sides to cover the entire back.

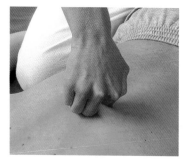

**4** Use your index and middle fingers to pinch and take hold of the tissue. Twist and lift the skin at the same time. Work within your partner's pain threshold. Cover the whole back using this technique.

# Improving digestion

 **If we are what we eat, then the healthy functioning of the digestive system is essential. Stress and tension are responsible for many digestive disturbances, including bloating, constipation, abdominal cramps, diarrhoea and indigestion.**

SHIATSU TREATMENTS

In shiatsu, the Stomach meridian is vital for the production of "ki" in the body. These movements help to relax the body and ease any digestive disturbances.

▸ **1** Sit at your partner's side and place your right hand on the stomach. Note the breathing rate: fast and shallow indicates tension. When you are attuned to your partner's breathing, continue.

**2** Using one hand on top of the other, apply pressure in a clockwise movement around the stomach. If you find tension, increase the pressure until it dissolves.

**3** With one hand on the other, rock and push from one side of the belly to the other, pulling back with the heel of the hand until you feel the stomach relax.

**4** Stretch your partner's leg out and place your knee or a pillow underneath your partner's knee for support. Apply palm pressure along the outside frontal edge of the leg following the Stomach meridian. Start from the top of the thigh and work down to the foot.

**5** Move down to your partner's feet and take a firm hold of the right ankle. Lean back and stretch the leg out. Repeat with the other leg. To finish the treatment, come back to the "hara" (abdomen) and tune in again, checking for any tension and relaxation of the muscles.

### REIKI INDIGESTION TREATMENT

These hand positions aid the digestion of food and can also help to free any blockages that are caused by emotional problems – often a cause of bad digestion.

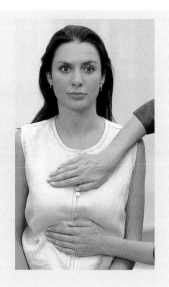

Kneel beside your partner and place one hand on the sternum and the other on the solar plexus at the centre or bottom of the rib-cage. If there is a stomach upset, constipation or diarrhoea, place the second hand lower down on the second chakra. Focus your attention and channel healing energy to the area.

# Relieving stress

**When we are under stress, the body pumps extra adrenalin in its "fight or flight" response. If this goes on for extended periods of time it has a damaging effect on our health and results in many common complaints.**

REFLEXOLOGY EASY BREATHING

When we are stressed, our breathing becomes quick and shallow and our digestion is upset. By breathing more deeply and slowly, we can help ourselves to cope with stress: it is not possible to panic while you are breathing well. This reflexology treatment works to open up the chest and lungs. It will calm you down, settle your nerves and increase the supply of life-giving oxygen to the body.

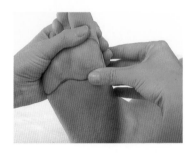

**1** Thumbwalk along the diaphragm line to release tension, pain and tightness. When it is contracting and relaxing freely, the abdominal organs are also stimulated.

**2** Work the lung reflexes on the chest area so that once the diaphragm is relaxed, the breathing can open up, increasing the supply of oxygen to the body.

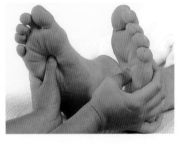

**3** Take both feet together and position your thumbs in the centre of the diaphragm line. As your partner breathes in, press in with your thumbs. Release as they breathe out. Repeat this several times.

SHIATSU SHOULDER MASSAGE
Stress causes the neck and shoul-ders to tighten, creating pain and stiffness. This treatment gives relief.

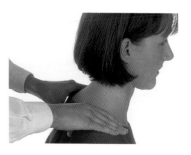

**1** Place your hands on your part-ner's shoulders and take a moment to tune in. Grip and hold the shoul-der muscles on each side of the neck. Squeeze them a few times in a rhythmic kneading action.

**2** Take a firm grip of the upper arms. Ask your partner to breathe in as you lift the shoulders up and breathe out as you allow the shoul-ders to drop back down again. Repeat the shoulder lift three times.

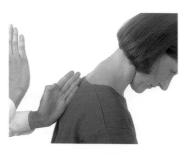

**3** Use a gentle hacking action with the sides of your hands. Move rhythmically across the shoulders and base of the neck. Keep the movement consistent, then increase the intensity as you feel the muscles relax.

**4** Place your forearms on your partner's shoulders. As you breathe out, press down with your arms on to the shoulders, applying gentle but firm, perpendicular, downward pressure. Repeat several times.

# Relieving tension

**Tension held in the body is usually the result of stress, pain or shock. The muscles tense or tighten up in an attempt to ward off the unpleasant stimuli. The healing touch of another's hands can help us to relax.**

HEAD AND NECK MASSAGE

When we feel tension, we usually hold it in our shoulders and neck, keeping ourselves taut. This unnatural posture can result in a thumping headache and aching around the eye area.

A good head massage helps the facial muscles relax and worry lines disappear. Your partner will feel fresher and may even look younger after receiving this highly effective tension-relieving treatment.

**1** Place your hands on the shoulders, fingers underneath and thumbs on top. Firmly massage the shoulders using a kneading action.

**2** Move your hands to the neck. With your thumbs on the side and fingers underneath, stretch out the neck by gently pulling away. Repeat several times.

**3** Lift your partner's head off the floor and firmly squeeze the muscles of the neck.

**4** Rub the scalp using your fingertips and then run your fingers through the hair.

**5** Using the fingers of both hands, work on the delicate facial tissue, moving symmetrically across the face to cover all the facial muscles.

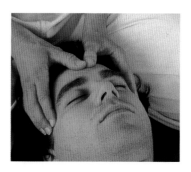

**6** Place the thumbs side by side on the centre of the forehead and stroke out to the temples, working in strips. Smooth any worry lines.

**7** Take the chin between thumb and fingers and gently pinch your way out along the jaw, relaxing and releasing any tension.

## TIPS FOR RELIEVING TENSION

• Take regular exercise to help diffuse tension and change the focus of your attention from any worries.

• Set aside some quiet time for yourself each day.
• Unwind in an aromatherapy bath before you go to sleep.

# Improving sleep

**A good night's sleep is essential for health. During sleep the body's cells renew and repair themselves and we relax. To prepare yourself for sleep, help the body to unwind before going to bed.**

RESTFUL SLEEP ENHANCER
A foot massage and reflexology treatment will help the body to relax. It will also improve the circulation and accelerate the removal of toxins. Try this treatment to make the most of the healing properties of sleep.

**1** Holding the foot with one hand, bring the foot down on to the thumb of your other hand and lift it off again. Move your thumb one step to the side and repeat, working your thumb methodically across the foot to the outer side, following the boundary line of the ball of the foot.

**2** Firmly thumbwalk along the diaphragm line. It is important to relax the diaphragm, because this area helps to calm the whole body and to steady the breathing.

▸ **3** Thumbwalk along the spinal reflex from the heel to the big toe. Support the outside of the foot with your other hand.

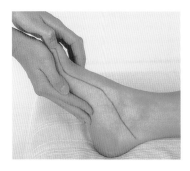

**4** Repeat, going down the spinal reflex several times. Rotate gently around any tight or sensitive areas.

**5** Gently thumbwalk up the back of the toes: do this with care as there is likely to be tenderness there.

AROMATIC HAND AND FOOT MASSAGE

Massaging the hands and feet will help to relax the whole body. Use small, circling strokes on the soles and palms, repeating the movements on the other foot and hand. Use firm pressure to avoid tickling and irritating movements.

## SLEEPY-TIME AROMAS

Try adding a few drops of essential oil to your massage oil or lotion.
• Lavender: for relaxing and balancing.
• Camomile: for soothing and calming.
• Neroli: for calming stress and anxiety.
• Clary sage or marjoram: for a strong sedative action.

# Looking after your hands

**We rely on our hands to perform countless everyday tasks. Our hands are one of the most overworked parts of the body, yet it is easy to take them for granted, forgetting to give them the care they deserve.**

SIMPLE HANDCARE

Everyday of our lives our environment has an impact on our hands. Freezing winter temperatures, biting winds, central heating, water, detergents and strong sunlight all have a damaging effect on the delicate skin of our hands. As we get older, our skin loses its elasticity and becomes increasingly dry.

There are a few simple things that we can do to look after our hands. Exposure to the sun is believed to be the main cause of skin aging, so it's essential to protect your hands from the damaging effect of the sun's harmful

▾ USE A MOISTURIZER CONTAINING A SUN-SCREEN TO PROTECT YOUR HANDS FROM ULTRAVIOLET LIGHT AND TO KEEP THE AGING EFFECTS OF THE SUN AT BAY.

## NAIL & HANDCARE TIPS

• To remove dead skin cells: add a teaspoon of salt to warm olive oil and massage into the hands.

• To strengthen the nails: rub a little neat lavender oil into the cuticles every night.

• For dry, brittle or weak nails, or nails with white flecks: make sure you have enough calcium, zinc and B vitamins.

ultraviolet rays: use a good-quality moisturizer containing ultraviolet filters. Get into the habit of wearing rubber gloves for washing up and always use a moisturizer after exposing them to water.

Age spots on the back of the hands are made worse by cold weather and sunlight. Protect your hands from wintry winds by investing in warm gloves, and use a richer moisturizer at this time of the year. Saffron oil or a few drops of lemon juice mixed into yogurt and rubbed into the hands can help to reduce age spots.

AROMATHERAPY PAMPERING TREATS
As well as looking after our hands on a day-to-day basis, a weekly manicure will keep the nails in good shape. Use essential oils to strengthen your nails.

**1** Soak your fingertips in either warm water, warm olive oil or use cider vinegar if the nails are weak. Gently clean the surplus cuticle from the nail area.

**2** Gently push the cuticles back with an orange stick wrapped in cotton wool. Use a cotton bud (Q-tip) to apply neat lavender oil to each cuticle.

▼ GOOD HAND CARE IS AS HELPFUL AN AID TO LOOKING YOUNG AS CARING FOR THE FACE.

▼ REGULARLY WASHING HANDS CAN DRY OUT THE SKIN, SO IT IS IMPORTANT TO MOISTURIZE.

# HEALING WITH
# YOGA AND
# MEDITATION

In the Sanskrit language, the word "yoga" refers
to union, harmony and balance. Beginning with
a look at our "five states of being", this chapter
shows how yoga can be used to heal, both
by rebalancing the nervous system and by
promoting the flow of energy through the body.
Through easily-learned postures (asanas), you
will see how habitual negativity can make way
for a positive relationship with the environment.

Yoga is often practised in conjunction with
meditation and the two share similar objectives:
to strengthen resolve and positive action through
a state of relaxed alertness. The meditations
recommended here can either be practised after
a yoga session, or in a quiet moment of the day.

# Healing and self-healing

**We all need healing, which simply means changing for the better at one or more levels of our being – the physical, energetic, nervous, thinking and attitudinal aspects. These five levels, called the koshas in yoga, are interactive.**

THE KOSHAS

These levels can be pictured as invisible layers, emanating outwards from the solid physical body (the first level). We feel the energy body as we approach someone or when they invade our space. The nervous system picks up signals from outside via our five senses. Our thoughts travel across space and even time. Our attitudes shape our destinies through eternity.

When we meditate we can become aware that these five levels of our being also flow inwards, contacting the vibrations of the spirit. These levels make up "who we are".

Successful healing brings us – the whole person – into our optimum state of harmony and well-being by treating not only our physical symptoms but also any energy disruptions, nervous imbalances, mental overload or deep

▶ TAKE TIME TO SIT STILL AND VISUALIZE THE KOSHAS EMANATING FROM YOUR PHYSICAL BODY.

physical level (red)

energetic level (orange/yellow)

above-conscious thinking level (blue)

below-conscious nervous level (green)

serene attitude level (violet)

▲ Practising yoga with your children creates a great sense of togetherness.

"soul sickness" that may be affecting us. This alters our whole outlook on life, even allowing us to live peacefully with symptoms or circumstances that previously caused us great distress.

## Self-healing with yoga

In yoga we take responsibility for our own well-being through the practice of self-discipline, self-awareness and self-surrender. Self-discipline simply means "sticking at it", practising yoga regularly, with enthusiasm and commitment. A few breaths and stretches here and there during quiet moments, plus a regular daily session of half-an-hour or so, is ideal – but any yoga is better than none at all and will still bring great results over time. Joining a weekly yoga class is a good idea and can inspire us to develop our practice further.

Self-awareness is essential for safety in practice. If anything feels wrong, stop doing it. Yoga is non-competitive, so we learn to know and accept how we feel today and to practise accordingly. Yoga is a state of relaxed alertness at all times. Self-surrender means letting go of our comfortable habits and familiar mindsets to make room for healthier ones. Our body lets go of its worn-out cells as new ones are formed. In the same way, we must let go of our worn-out opinions, prejudices, habits, self-image and other burdens.

# The nervous system

**The nervous system is related to the middle kosha that links our physical and energetic states (or "body" koshas) with the thinking and attitudinal levels (or "mind" koshas). The system has several branches; yoga works on them all.**

The middle kosha contains all the unconscious aspects of the mind, such as the memory, instinct, and programmed responses, as well as the nervous system that allows the conscious mind to communicate with the body and

▼ Yoga teaches us that we can consciously choose when to relax.

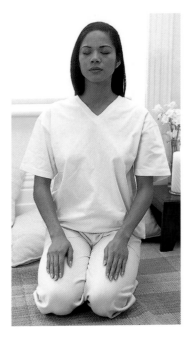

to turn thoughts into physical actions. The brain and spinal cord provide the main "motorway" for nervous impulses to travel along the nerve cells to and from all parts of the body. It is vital to keep this "traffic" flowing freely.

Yoga makes us more aware through the sensory nervous system: our sight, hearing, touch, taste and smell become more alert and responsive. It makes us more skilful in movement through the motor nervous system, which tells each muscle when to contract and by how much. It even allows us to access the autonomic nervous system, so that we can choose consciously when to be keyed up or relaxed while maintaining our inner serenity.

THE AUTONOMIC NERVOUS SYSTEM
This system maintains homeostasis (internal harmony) by controlling the respiratory, cardiovascular, digestive, hormonal, immune and other involuntary body systems.

Its two complementary branches work together like the accelerator and brakes in a car. One branch "revs up" certain systems to help us deal with imminent physical danger. This is known as the "fright-fight-flight" response and it is needed for surviving external threats. The other branch deals with nourishment, long-term maintenance, rest and repair. It is responsible for ensuring our longer-term health and survival. Most of us fail to appreciate that we do not have the resources to attend to both these aspects at the same time. If we spend too much time in fight-or-flight mode, we are neglecting to digest our food or repair our damaged cells, and tiredness and poor health will inevitably follow.

Our nervous systems have not yet evolved to cope with the profound changes in lifestyle wrought by our technological society, which is only about 200 years old. Today, our lives are highly stressful, competitive and go-getting, making us feel angry, frustrated, confused and anxious a lot of the time, and it is not surprising that many of us get

▲ KEEP YOUR SPINE LOOSE AND SUPPLE TO HELP YOUR NERVOUS SYSTEM DO ITS WORK.

stuck in the fright-fight-flight syndrome. Since there is no physical enemy for us to kill or escape from, the stress hormones in our bodies remain unused. These can build up to dangerous levels and eventually lead to serious diseases. Our nervous systems may become totally out of balance, with the accelerator on full throttle nearly all the time.

The autonomic nervous system may seem to be beyond our conscious control, but fortunately we can influence it through yoga, helping us to regain internal harmony and balance.

# The spine's energy motorway

**The spine houses a subtle "motorway" that carries the life force in our energy body. As it enters or leaves at the "roundabouts" or chakras, this life force is a blend of all our energies: physical, vital, nervous, mental and attitudinal.**

If the spine's energy "motorway" is obstructed the "side roads" become blocked and their territory is deprived of essential nourishment, communications, and the ability to remove toxic wastes. The resulting distress is called "illness". You can keep the traffic flowing smoothly in the spine through the use of posture, movements with breath awareness, visualization, relaxation and meditation.

### THE CHAKRAS

Energy enters and leaves our spine through the chakras. These are also associated with the three important cavities in our bodies. The abdominal cavity protects our vital organs and houses three major chakras dealing with the energies of Life: survival, social interaction and self-confidence. The legs and feet are extensions of our survival chakra. Great emphasis is placed in yoga upon strengthening the lower body so that we can cope with the challenges of living.

The skull cavity lies at the top of the spine and protects the brain. It houses two major chakras concerned with the energies of

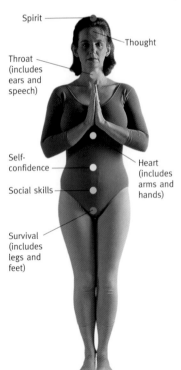

Spirit

Thought

Throat (includes ears and speech)

Self-confidence

Social skills

Heart (includes arms and hands)

Survival (includes legs and feet)

◄ THE CHAKRAS REPRESENT THE THREE ENERGIES OF LIFE, LIGHT AND LOVE.

▲ *SAVASANA* IS A CLASSIC EXAMPLE
OF SPINAL ALIGNMENT.

awareness and wisdom or Light. Breathing and balancing exercises switch on the Light in our heads, giving us greater understanding in both yoga and daily life.

Lying between the skull and abdominal cavities is the thoracic cavity. This protects our hearts and lungs and houses the two chakras concerned with relationship or Love energies. The arms and hands are extensions of the heart chakra (for reaching out to others) and the ears and mouth are extensions of the throat chakra (for communicating). Simply thinking about someone engages relationship (Love) energies, even if we don't actually like them. Yoga gradually increases our capacity for unconditional love and cancels out negative thoughts and feelings. Backbends and chest expanding exercises help to open and lift the upper body, allowing Love energy to flow more freely. It also improves our breathing and circulation.

▶ IN *TADASANA*, YOU ARE ALIGNING YOUR
SPINE WHILE FIGHTING THE FORCES OF
GRAVITY. IT IS A SIMPLE YET STRONG POSE.

# Breathing patterns

**Yoga helps us to change our breathing. Slow, deep breathing through the nose relaxes the heart and sends "all is well" messages to the brain. Once we have learned yoga breathing habits we can lessen our stress and anxiety.**

A fast, shallow breathing pattern, with panting or gasping through the mouth to "snatch" more air, is usually the result of stress. This type of breathing strains the heart and makes the stress worse. It also sends panic messages to the brain, which then revs up the fright-fight-flight response and a vicious circle is created: "Quick! Fight harder! Run away faster!" Since we cannot physically fight the boss nor flee from a traffic jam, we end up feeling even more anxious and stressed.

The diaphragm is the chief "breathing muscle". It lies across the base of the chest, separating it from the abdomen above the waist (and stomach). When we breathe in, it flattens downwards, massaging the abdominal organs. When we breathe out it relaxes upwards into the chest. "Deep" yoga breathing is diaphragmatic breathing. In yoga postures the breath is co-ordinated with both stretching and moving energy.

KNEELING POSE, *VAJRASANA*

▲ Sit on your heels, with big toes touching underneath you. Tuck your tailbone under and tilt your pelvis backwards, to avoid hollowing your lumbar spine. Clasp your hands in your lap and stretch the spine up, lifting and opening your chest. Keep your chin and shoulders down. Breathe slowly and deeply a few times in this position and focus on feeling the breathing movements within.

ARM AND CHEST STRETCH
WITH BREATH

BODY-MIND BREATHING CYCLE

Now add the feeling of moving energy up and down the spine, which calms, balances and heals the nervous system. The general rule is to move energy upwards through the spine on the breath IN and to stretch and energize the limbs on the breath OUT. You may need several breaths to perfect a posture. End by breathing OUT to bring energy down and relax.

▲ Sit in *vajrasana* (see opposite). Now, as you breathe IN, kneel up and stretch your clasped hands directly overhead, with your palms up. Breathe OUT and stretch up even more. Breathe IN to sit on heels and OUT to lower hands to lap. Repeat the sequence a few times, co-ordinating breath and movements. The arm stretch, with the breath, can also be done when standing or sitting on a chair.

▲ Put palms together with your elbows out to the side. Stand in a comfortable upright position. Pull the spine up and breathe IN, squeezing the inner thighs and pelvic floor muscles. Breathe OUT, squeezing corset muscles at waist. Breathe IN, pressing palms together and squeezing spinal muscles behind the heart to lift and open the chest. Breathe OUT to relax. Repeat three times.

# Spinal alignment

**Good spinal posture is vital to the health and well-being of all five koshas. It allows free passage of nervous impulses between the body cells and the brain, and of vital energy within and between the chakras.**

DANGERS OF POOR POSTURE

Many common health problems are linked to poor posture. Besides causing compression in certain nerve pathways and disharmony in the chakras, poor posture also causes physical problems around the areas where the spine is out of alignment. Blockages in the structural, nervous or energy systems will reveal themselves in time through congestion, distress, pain and eventually disease around the area involved.

COMMON PROBLEMS

Rigidity in the pelvic and sacral area puts pressure on the hip, knee, ankle and foot joints, and the ligaments. This pressure eventually makes movement, and walking, difficult and painful.

▾ DO YOU RECOGNIZE ANY OF THESE COMMON POSTURAL PROBLEMS IN YOURSELF?

Compression of the digestive organs results in insufficient oxygenated blood causing them to malfunction. This can lead to infection as the stale blood is not removed.

Compression of the cervical spine (causing a jutting chin) is a frequent cause of headaches and mouth breathing, which can itself cause nasal and sinus congestion.

A weakness in the thoracic spine (which causes a concave chest) can result in the compression of the diaphragm and intercostal muscles. This can lead to poor breathing, chest infections, lung congestion and heart and circulation problems.

Compression in the lumbar spine (caused largely by weak abdominal muscles) results in all kinds of lower back and leg pain (including trapped nerves and sciatica) and failure to hold the

▲ WHEN STANDING CORRECTLY, THE BODY IS BALANCED AND THE SPINE STRETCHED UP.

lower organs in place. This can lead to problems such as prolapse and incontinence.

Some problems are caused by structural abnormalities, and yoga can often help. Most of the above problems, however, are due to poor posture, which is apt to deteriorate further with age or excessive weight gain. Fortunately, they can be halted and even reversed through gentle and persistent yoga practice, especially those practices that improve spinal alignment through movement and isometric "muscle squeezing" done standing, kneeling, sitting or lying.

The chakras, or vitality centres, can also be energized and balanced when breathing and visualization practices are combined with an awareness of spinal alignment. A strong lower body allows the upper body to lift and open.

# Improving posture

**This isometric "muscle-squeezing" exercise will improve your posture. Do it lying on your back, sitting, kneeling or standing. Practise it anywhere and often, to replace poor postural habits with good ones.**

ISOMETRIC EXERCISE

**1** Stretch up through your spine. Press the palms together at heart level before lifting your elbows to shoulder height.

**2** Begin by tightening the muscles of the inner thighs (at the top near the groin). Involve the backs of the thighs as well, but keep the buttocks relaxed. Squeeze an actual or imaginary jar between the thighs. These muscles help to support the trunk when standing.

**3** Next tighten the pelvic floor muscles. These muscles also help to support the weight of the trunk. Squeeze as though pulling the base of the body up inside. Weakness in the pelvic floor muscles causes lower back pain, sexual problems and also incontinence (especially after childbirth).

▼ ISOMETRIC EXERCISE INVOLVES ALMOST IMPERCEPTIBLE BUT POWERFUL MOVEMENTS.

**4** Now tilt the pelvis slightly by tucking the tailbone under. Lift the pubic bone by tightening the lower abdominal and groin muscles. These muscles help to hold the sacral spine in alignment, correcting excess lumbar curvature and pressure on the sacroiliac joints.

**5** Tighten the corset muscles (the transverse abdominals), pulling the waist and navel back towards the spine. This holds the lumbar spine in place and prevents abdominal sagging. Your energy will sweep spontaneously up through your chest, neck, head and crown, as you realign them by opening the chest, lifting the ears away from the shoulders and bringing the head in line with the spine.

**6** The muscles on each side of the thoracic spine hold it upright and

▲ TIGHTENING THE CORSET MUSCLES KEEPS THE TORSO ERECT AND ENERGY FLOWING.

keep the chest open. Pressing the palms hard together activates these muscles and lifts the chest. Breathe IN strongly, drawing your energy down from the crown, bringing Light into your body and mind, and opening yourself to the Love energies radiating from within your "divine core".

### WATCHPOINT
Do not squeeze the pelvic floor or abdominal muscles if you are pregnant, after recent abdominal surgery or have serious digestive problems. Instead, focus on lifting up through the lower, middle and upper spine.

**7** To release this posture, breathe OUT slowly and deeply. Take your energy down to your feet then relax, releasing all physical, mental and emotional "waste products". Let them become neutralized by the Earth. Do three rounds only. Repeat this exercise frequently.

# Letting go

**Deep relaxation is an essential part of yoga practice, whether it is a short rest between exercises or fifteen blissful minutes ending with your resolve, or *sankalpa*. The shoulders and hips hold tension and should be eased first.**

MAKING A RESOLVE

We feel happy and at peace when we relax. We can retain this feeling afterwards by changing some of our unhelpful attitudes towards life while we are in the relaxed state. If life is a journey we can choose either to "climb mountains" (difficulty and struggle) or to "go with the flow" (relaxing and letting go). It is up to us, but making room for change means letting go of negative or outdated beliefs and trusting the Cosmos (or God, the Universal Life Force or Spirit) to guide us into the future.

SANKALPA

Meaning "resolve", *sankalpa* is a yoga practice for changing our attitudes. We can change the energies in any of our chakras, building up more vitality (Life), awareness (Light) or positive attitudes in our relationships (Love) by practising *sankalpa* in deep relaxation.

Before entering into relaxation, we choose how we want to be and

▲ THE BUTTERFLY STRETCH IS A RELAXING POSE FOR DEEP BREATHING AND LOOSENING THE HIP JOINTS.

form a statement in simple words, starting with phrases such as "From this moment on I am becoming more and more …" or "I am feeling more and more …" or simply "I am …". Use only positive words that make you feel good about yourself. Be positive. Avoid words that suggest the possibility of failure, such as "try", or words that reinforce your present condition, such as "less tired/negative/depressed" and so on. Avoid projecting into the future with statements saying "I will be/feel/become …", remembering that change can only happen in the here and now.

Choose only one quality at a time for your *sankalpa*, and stick with it until it is no longer needed. Repeat the same *sankalpa* every time you relax, also upon waking and before going to sleep. Meanwhile live your life as if you already have the quality you are developing. When your *sankalpa* is established, make a new one.

### *SAVASANA*, CORPSE POSE

This is a great relaxation position and is called the corpse pose because all the muscles relax. Your body temperature will drop, so you may need a light blanket.

## SANKALPA AFFIRMATIONS

You may find the following *sankalpas* helpful:

**Life**: *From this moment on I am becoming stronger/healthier/ healed/more confident/more positive about my life.*

**Light**: *I am more aware, more understanding, more perceptive ... Or, I am learning new skills and new attitudes.*

**Love**: *I am feeling more and more peaceful/happy/positive/ relaxed/contented/balanced/ accepting of my situation. Or, I am forgiving of myself and/or other people.*

**1** Roll the feet and hips in and out to find the best position, then roll the hands and shoulders in and out. If your chin juts up, place a small cushion under your head.

**2** If your waist arches away from the ground, place a cushion under your knees. It takes time and awareness to find and settle into your most relaxed position.

# How to practise yoga

**We practise yoga techniques – posture, breathing, movements with breath and energy flow, classical poses, relaxation, resolve and meditation – in order to become "yogic" and to live daily life in the state or attitude of "yoga".**

YOGA MEANS UNION

Both yoga and true healing involve creating harmony between the five koshas – the physical, energetic, nervous, thinking and attitudinal levels of our being. The result is more abundant Life (energy), Light (awareness) and Love (receiving and giving).

WHAT YOU NEED FOR PRACTICE

Choose a quiet warm space, with enough room to lie down and stretch. Wear loose clothing. Have a rug or shawl handy for relaxation and meditation. It is best to work on a non-slip mat or piece of carpet, roughly 180cm x 60cm (6ft x 2ft) and use a firm cushion or upright chair to sit on for breathing and meditation. Some extra small cushions are also useful.

Set aside a regular time and place each day, to establish your "yoga habit". Practise yoga before eating, with an empty bladder and bowels. Wait about two hours after a large meal.

WHICH TECHNIQUES TO PRACTISE

Always involve all five koshas, however short your practice. Begin with a breathing exercise and careful spinal alignment to harmonize the nervous system. Continue with some stretches to release physical tension and get your energy flowing. End with relaxation and/or meditation to relax your mind and release negativity. Repeat your *sankalpa* (see earlier in this chapter) for healing, and to create beneficial changes in attitude.

▼ GATHER TOGETHER EQUIPMENT TO SUPPORT YOU IN YOUR POSTURES.

▲ Simple movements release tension and encourage energy to flow.

Several sequences are shown for you to "mix and match" to suit your energy levels. Choose to lie, sit or kneel if you feel weak or tired. When you feel energetic practise vigorously while standing, in order to develop strength and stamina. Rest briefly between sequences and for longer at the end. Practice should be regular rather than long: 15–30 minutes once or twice a day is ideal, plus a weekly yoga class if possible.

Every day is different and yoga brings improvements very quickly. Your own body is your best guide. Practise at what is a comfortable pace for you today, and for only as long as the exertion is enjoyable. If you feel breathless or shaky, take a rest and slow down your breathing. Resume your practice later when you feel better, perhaps choosing an easier sequence.

Make yoga part of your life
Stay focused in your yogic attitude, whatever you are doing. Use odd moments for stretching, alignment, breathing or repeating your resolve – waiting for the kettle to boil, after long sitting or telephoning. There are many such moments in a day.

▼ Yoga can be practised whenever you have a moment to spare.

# Getting started

**Start your yoga practice lying down if you feel stiff, tired or unwell. Allow gravity to help and support you as you breathe slowly and deeply and limber up gently to get your circulation and energy flowing. You will soon feel great.**

BE GENTLE WITH YOURSELF

Before you start, make sure that you are comfortable. Use pillows or cushions if you need support. If you are feeling unwell or are recovering from illness, take things very easy. If in doubt, consult your health practitioner before starting – but remember that yoga can work wonders at many levels, even if "exercise" is contra-indicated.

BREATHING

Lie comfortably, with knees bent and head supported if necessary. Feel your energy moving as you breathe, travelling up through your body as you breathe IN, and down again as you breathe OUT. Let your

▼ *SAVASANA* IS A TRADITIONAL YOGA POSE – IDEAL FOR GENTLE EXERCISE WHEN UNWELL.

▲ USE YOGA TO DISPEL SLUGGISHNESS AND GET YOUR CIRCULATION MOVING.

breath soften and lengthen as you connect with the "tide of life" and float upon it for a few moments.

MOVING THE EXTREMITIES

Before you begin the postures, flex and stretch your fingers and toes, then your ankles and wrists. Move your feet and hands in circles in every yoga session and at odd moments during the day. Moving the extremities is the easiest and quickest technique to get the circulation and energy moving through the whole body. Practised regularly, this helps to remove congestion, stagnation, sluggish-ness and fluid retention, and wakes up the nervous system.

### Pelvic lift

▲ Lie on your back with knees bent. Breathe IN to tighten pelvic floor and lower abdominal muscles. Breathe OUT to tilt pelvis and tuck tailbone under. Breathe IN to lift pelvis. Breathe OUT to lower. Repeat.

### Knees to chest

▲ Lie on your back and clutch your knees to your chest. Hug with your arms and lift your head gently to your knees. Roll gently from side to side, then vigorously forward and back to sit up.

### Lying twist

▲ Lie on your back with knees bent. Keep ankles, knees and inner thighs pressed together through-out. These muscles support the groin, pelvic floor and lower spine. Breathe OUT to lower the knees to the floor. Breathe IN to raise them (still pressed together). Repeat.

### Seated forward bend

▲ Place your head over bent knees and gradually stretch out your legs. Keep your spine long and relaxed. Breathe deeply into the back of your chest a few times. Breathe IN to move energy up the spine and OUT to move it down. Unfold and return to *savasana* to relax.

# Energy and balance

These sequences charge you with energy (Life) and wake up your mind (Light). Use them to start the day, or after too much mental work or enforced sitting. Always practise yoga in bare feet – unless stretching in public places!

DYNAMIC STANDING WARM-UP

Simply walking about on tiptoe is one of the best energizers there is. Standing on your toes strengthens your feet and ankles and relieves congestion, stagnation and fluid retention in the legs (Life). To stand on tiptoe and look up calls for balancing skills that sharpen the brain (Light). If your sight or hearing is impaired you will find balancing a challenge, so hold on to something, or practise with your back against a wall for support.

▼ STANDING ON TIPTOE STRENGTHENS MUSCLES AND SHARPENS THE MIND.

SQUATTING

To begin squatting, try leaning against a wall for support. Keep your heels a little way away from the wall to help you balance.

▲ Stand with your feet apart and hands on hips. Align the spine and tighten the muscles of the lower trunk. Breathe OUT as you bend your knees to the sides and lower into a squat, keeping your spine upright. Breathe IN as you rise to standing again. Avoid bending forward as you lower yourself down – hold on to the edge of a table if needed.

## STANDING STRETCH

Stretching your arms overhead strengthens the chest muscles and opens the chest to allow better breathing. Keep your spine aligned and your arms well back, in line with your shoulders, to stretch the pectoral muscles and lift the sternum. Poor posture, fatigue and depression shorten these muscles and reduce the lung area. This worsens the poor breathing that created these problems in the first place. If, when you stretch your arms overhead, you feel breathless (through weakness or chest or heart problems), practise this exercise with your hands in *namaste* (prayer position) at heart level.

**1** Stand tall, aligning your spine and distributing the weight evenly on both feet. Tighten the muscles of the lower trunk (Life) for strength to stretch up and open chest (Love).

**2** Breathe IN, raising arms to sides and overhead, and coming on to your toes. Breathe OUT to lower arms and heels. Repeat vigorously until glowing with energy.

# Positive feelings

**These arm-circling, side-bending and twisting movements should all be done while keeping the lower body strong and unmoving and the spine in alignment. The movement is all from the waist upwards, in the thoracic area (Love).**

OPENING THE CHEST FROM
A STRONG BASE

These movements should be able to cheer up the gloomiest and most lethargic person, since they cleanse the lungs, improve the circulation and open the heart centre. Stand firmly with feet about hip-width apart, arches and inner knees lifted, back and inner thighs strong, pelvic floor drawn up, abdominal muscles holding the pelvis and spine in good alignment.

As you practise the movements, take your attention and your energy right into your fingertips. They are extensions of your loving heart, reaching out to embrace the world and everyone in it, including yourself. Feel that streamers of light are flowing out from your fingers in big circles up, down and around you, brightening up the atmosphere as you stretch and move through your whole body. For a less energetic version, the movements can also be done while kneeling or sitting cross-legged.

ARM CIRCLING

**1** Stand with feet about hip-width apart and arms out to sides.

**2** Breathe IN to raise arms forward and up. Breathe OUT to lower them back and down. Repeat several times, making big circles.

## Chest opening

**1** Stand tall with feet apart and arms in front at shoulder level. Keep your shoulders down and neck long throughout.

**2** Breathe IN to take straight arms to sides at shoulder level. Breathe OUT to return them to the front. Repeat vigorously.

## Side bending

## Rotating trunk

▲ Stand with feet apart. Breathe IN, stretching your spine up. Breathe OUT to bend to the right, keeping the left shoulder back and in line. Repeat to left. Repeat both sides.

▲ Standing with feet apart, swing the arms and rotate the upper trunk from side to side, keeping the spine upright, the arms loose and breathing naturally and vigorously.

# Breathing exercises

**Yogic breathing removes stress. With practice, we can learn to de-stress ourselves in almost any situation, simply by breathing through the nose and engaging the diaphragm in slow, deep breathing movements for a few moments.**

Shallow, stress-related breathing emphasizes the top and middle parts of the chest, similar to when we are panting from unexpected exertion such as running for a bus. Peaceful, rhythmical breathing engages the lower part of the chest and especially the diaphragm.

Yogic three-part breathing uses all the breathing muscles around the bottom, middle and top of the lungs. Stand, sit or lie and settle your breathing before you start. Just three deep yogic breaths may be enough to trigger the "all is well" response when we are feeling

### THE YOGIC THREE-PART BREATH

**1** Place your hands on your waist to feel the movement of the diaphragm and lower ribs as you breathe deeply IN and OUT.

**2** Now place your hands around the sides and front of the chest and feel the ribs opening and the

sternum (breastbone) rising as you breathe IN. Breathe OUT and feel them retracting.

**3** Then move your hands to your collarbones. As you breathe IN fully you may feel them move slightly.

**4** Breathe IN from the base of the lungs to feel as though your chest cavity is filling with air up to the collarbones. Breathe OUT as fully and slowly as possible (residual air always remains in the lungs) to release tension.

stressed. This is the quickest and easiest way to control our nervous system and to calm it down when our mind and emotions have revved it up.

All yoga techniques exercise and relax mind and body. *Alternate nostril breathing* also restores the balance between them. Being too introverted makes us depressed or mentally exhausted and being too extroverted makes us physically exhausted. Mind and body are designed to work in harmony. People who spend too much time "in their heads" as well as those undergoing physical exhaustion, trauma or a life crisis, can benefit greatly from this simple exercise, followed by deep relaxation. You need to practise it on a day-to-day basis though, before turning to it in a crisis. Build up the number of rounds very gradually.

### ALTERNATE NOSTRIL BREATHING

**1** Sit erect on a chair. Place index and middle finger of right hand on forehead with left hand in lap. Close right nostril with thumb and breathe IN through open left nostril. Close left nostril with ring finger and open right nostril. Breathe OUT through open right nostril.

**2** Breathe IN through open right nostril. Close it with your thumb and open left nostril. Breathe OUT through left nostril. This is one round. Do several rounds then rest a moment with natural breathing, and observe how you feel. Repeat several times.

# Balancing stretches

**The focus here is on keeping the spine stretched and aligned all along its length while holding your balance – whether standing on one leg or both – and performing the different movements with deep concentration.**

These stretches all require balance, focus and concentration, so they are good for Light energies (the mind). They also require a strong lower body (Life) and with regular practise, help you gain an open chest with relaxed arms, shoulders and neck (Love).

ISOMETRIC BALANCING

**1** Stand with hands clasped and head bowed. Breathe IN to focus on tightening inner thigh and pelvic floor muscles. Breathe OUT as you raise arms to the sides a little and focus on squeezing "corset" muscles around the navel, pulling the navel back towards the spine.

**2** Breathe IN as you rise on to your toes, raising your arms high to the sides and opening the chest by focusing on and squeezing the muscles along the upper spine. Breathe OUT to relax arms, feet, head and squeezed muscles. Do three rounds.

## CHEST AND THIGH STRETCH

## LOOSENING ROLLING TWIST

⬆ Rolling twists are energetic, so do them slowly and with awareness and stop if your breathing speeds up. Stand with feet about 75cm (2½ft) apart and hands on hips. Stretch up through the spine and push the pelvis forward with knees loose as you breathe IN. Breathe OUT to lean back from the upper trunk. Twist forward and clockwise in a fluid motion. Breathe naturally, focusing on maintaining strength and stillness in the lower body, with all the movement from the waist and upper spine. After a few rounds, repeat anticlockwise.

⬆ Stand on one leg and bend the other knee, holding the foot against your buttock with the bent elbow pointing back. Raise your other hand high in front, as though pressing it against a wall. It is helpful to practise this pose while standing about 15cm (6in) away from a wall, so that you have to stretch up and really open the chest.

# The tree pose

**This sequence is excellent for spinal alignment and energy flow, as well as working the abdominal muscles. It works the legs strongly, opens the chest, raises the arms and engages the optical and balancing mechanisms in the brain.**

STANDING IN THE TREE POSE
Nearly all the classical *asanas* (yoga poses) work on all the energy centres along the spine, and the tree pose is a good example.

**1** Stand with your feet hip-width apart and parallel, toes evenly spread. Feeling rooted to the floor, allow your right leg to float up, bent at the knee. Take hold of your right foot and position the sole firmly against the inner thigh of your strong, standing leg, with the bent knee out to the side, feeling the opening in the hip joint.

**2** If you cannot achieve this position, place the sole wherever comfortable on the inside of the straight leg – what is important is to keep the knee back so as to open up the hip area. Realign your pelvis, tucking your tailbone under, and softly fix your gaze on a point in front of you to help you balance. When you feel steady, join your palms in *namaste*, breathing freely. Hold the position for several breaths, then breathe OUT to bring the leg and arms neatly down. Repeat the movement with the opposite leg.

**3** Feel how the muscles on either side of your leg and trunk are working together, co-operating in the job of holding you upright and steady. Come out of the pose if you start to wobble. Once you feel rooted and secure in this pose, raise your arms slowly overhead, palms together, breathing in. Breathe deeply and hold the pose. Repeat on the other side.

## WATCHPOINT
If balance is a problem, lean against a wall and experiment with the position of the bent leg until you find the best stance.

**4** When you have worked equally on both sides, stand calmly to settle your body and breath. When you are ready, breathe IN to raise your arms over your head, being careful not to arch the lower back. Stretch right through from your heels to your fingertips and take a few breaths. Then breathe OUT to bend your knees as though you are sitting down. Keeping your spine as vertical as possible, lower yourself until you are almost squatting. Keep your heels on the floor. Take a few deep breaths in this position, then breathe IN to stand again. Repeat this "standing seat" several times.

# Forward and backward bends

**Many people bend forward by stretching their lumbar spine, with rigid hips and knees. This puts great strain on a very vulnerable area. Practising correct forward and backward bends gives you greater flexibility and a fully stretched back.**

## PREPARATION

This sequence is strong and dynamic. It requires some limbering movements first, especially in the upper spine, such as *opening the chest*. Movements such as *dynamic standing warm-ups* or *squatting*, strengthen the legs and feet and make the hips, knees and ankles more flexible. *Squatting* also trains the spine to remain upright when you are bending down.

## PROTECTING THE LOWER BACK

Bending incorrectly – usually from the lumbar spine – is the most frequent cause of lower backache, especially when lifting. When you practise any kind of standing forward bend in your yoga sessions, first tighten your spine-supporting muscles and always bend forward with knees well bent and spine as straight as possible.

Your upper trunk and head are very heavy, especially if you let them sag like dead weights – so stretch the spine out and forward

▲ LIMBER UP FOR THE BENDS BY LIFTING YOUR KNEES TO STRENGTHEN LEGS AND HIPS.

as you bend from the hips and take your body weight into your strong thighs. Your spine is precious and you can protect it by developing both awareness and lower body strength. Bend forward only as far as you can. Place your hands on your shins, ankles or the floor to support your upper body weight before attempting to straighten your knees. It is more important to stretch your spine than your legs.

### Forward bending

Experiment with picking up a light but bulky box from a squatting position and then rise by straightening your legs – there should be no stretching in your lumbar spine (below and behind the waist) because your legs are strong enough to lift the weight of both your own body and the box. The muscles that hold your spine in place, which you have been strengthening through sessions of *body-mind breathing,* are protecting your lower back at all times. While in a forward bending position, with knees well bent and your head hanging down, you can release tension in your neck and shoulders by gently rotating your head.

### Standing forward bend

**1** Stand with feet about 75cm (2½ft) apart and knees well bent. Breathe OUT to bend forward and clasp your ankles or shins. Breathe IN. Breathe OUT to relax and let the spine lengthen, keeping legs bent.

**2** On each breath OUT let gravity stretch your spine more, to get your best stretch for today. Finally straighten your legs if you can. Roll up very gently and stretch your arms up.

### Backward bending

The aim is to increase flexibility in the thoracic spine (chest) without overarching the lumbar spine or the neck (cervical spine). Chest expansion exercises are a good way to do this. Practise this movement frequently as it's very good at relieving feelings of tightness and for improving breathing capacity. It is also a good way to warm up your spine before the back bends.

The neck carries all the nerves from the brain to the body. Congestion here is often caused by hunched shoulders, as we unconsciously attempt to "carry the world on our shoulders". Dropping the

### Chest expansion

**1** Stand tall and clasp your hands behind your back. Breathe OUT as you straighten your arms and lift them up behind you, keeping your lower body firm. Breathe IN to return your arms and stretch up through your spine.

**2** Breathe OUT to bend the upper spine backwards, keeping your knees bent and lifting your straight arms up behind you. Take a few breaths in this position. Breathe IN to straighten up. Drop your head back only if it feels comfortable.

shoulders and opening the chest, as in back-bending poses, relieves this congestion, which is a common cause of headaches and feelings of acute tension. People who look and feel uptight are apt to have stiff shoulders, necks and thoracic spines because they are habitually "holding themselves together".

## WATCHPOINT

The head is very heavy, so decide whether or not to drop it back. If your neck feels at all weak or uncomfortable, just look up and raise your chin as you bend backwards. As you come upright, lower your chin very slowly.

### STANDING BACK BEND

**3** Breathe OUT to bend forwards with knees bent, lifting your straight arms up behind you. Take a few breaths in this position. Breathe IN to straighten up. Repeat this sequence frequently to open the chest and improve posture.

**1** Stand with hands on waist or lower back. Breathe IN and stand tall. Breathe OUT, pushing pelvis forward, bending knees and arching upper spine backwards. Remember to take a few breaths. Breathe IN to come up slowly.

# Twisting the spine

Spinal twists stimulate and strengthen the muscles on either side of the spine. These hold it in alignment by working equally on both sides. They also increase flexibility by contracting on one side and releasing on the other.

PREPARATION

Before twisting the spine extend it fully and avoid leaning forward or back. This allows the spine to twist from the waist upwards through the thoracic and cervical areas, opening the chest and stimulating the nerves that radiate outwards from the upper spine. A spine that is not fully stretched will twist too much in the lumbar area, rather than evenly along its whole length.

This imbalance is a common cause of backache. Practise twisting movements after warming up well.

HELPING THE HEART AND CIRCULATION

All movement helps the heart and circulation (especially the diaphragm's movement when breathing slowly and deeply). Twisting movements also help to flush out the "used up" blood and toxic waste products that result

SIMPLE SEATED TWIST

**1** Sit tall, with your legs in front and your hands beside you. Place the sole of the left foot on the floor on the far side of the right leg. Breathe IN and stretch your spine up.

**2** Breathe OUT to bring your right arm over the left knee and take hold of your right leg for leverage. Breathe IN to stretch up. Breathe OUT to twist. Repeat other side.

from energy production in the cells, and to get freshly oxygenated blood to every cell – especially in parts of the body that can be hard to reach in other ways.

### Stretching the spine

First practise three rounds of *body-mind breathing* to tighten the muscles that support the spine. Keeping your mind on these muscles and the spine stretched up, breathe OUT and twist. This squeezes stale blood out of areas that can get congested – the abdominal organs, spinal muscles, lungs and neck. As you breathe in again and untwist, freshly oxygenated blood rushes into the areas that you have just squeezed.

### Forward twisting

**1** Stand with feet about 75cm (2½ft) apart and arms stretched out in front of you at shoulder height. Breathe IN. Breathe OUT and bring the right hand down your right leg and your left hand up above you in a straight line.

**2** Turn your head (if comfortable) to look at your left hand. Breathe IN to straighten up into starting position. Breathe OUT to bring left hand to left leg. Repeat vigorously. For more twist, slide your hand down your opposite leg instead.

# Kneeling sequence

**Kneeling or sitting is less tiring than standing, because gravity is with you rather than against you. These yoga poses work to loosen your upper back and shoulders, as well as your knees and ankles.**

PREPARATION

Sit on your heels, with big toes turned in to touch each other. If your knees are stiff, place a cushion between your shins and your ankles. If your ankles are stiff, place a cushion beneath them until you are more flexible.

CHILD POSE

⌃ Sit on your heels and breathe IN. Breathe OUT to bend forward. Place your forehead on the floor, bringing your arms close to your feet. If your chest or bust feels compressed, you may prefer to rest your forehead on your fists or on a cushion. Breathe into your ribs at the back to expand your breathing for a few moments.

FLEXIBILITY IN THE LOWER BODY

Stiffness indicates poor circulation, usually due to lack of movement. Our skeletal and muscular systems are designed for movement – animals move from place to place and human "animals" have learnt to move on two legs, freeing the upper limbs. However, this puts great strain on the pelvis and lower back because they bear the body's whole weight. Yoga helps alleviate congestion, pressure and pain in the lower half of the body.

STRENGTH IN THE UPPER BODY

The upper spine, shoulders and arms are also often out of balance because they do not carry enough weight to keep them strong. Again, yoga brings our awareness to this tendency. Bearing the body weight more equally in the all-fours position allows us to regain flexibility and relieve strain and congestion in the lower back, and develop greater strength in the muscles of the upper trunk.

## Cat stretch

## Back arch

**1** Sitting on your heels, stretch your hands forward along the floor, then raise your buttocks so that your shoulders are over your wrists and your hips are over your knees. Stretch out your fingers to make a broad base to take your weight. Breathe IN with your back flat and your neck relaxed.

⏶ Sit on your heels with your big toes turned in and touching. Place your hands on the floor behind you with fingers pointing towards your buttocks. Spread your fingers and lean back with your wrists under your shoulders. Breathe IN, lifting the chest high. Breathe OUT to lower the chest. Repeat.

**2** Breathe OUT as you arch your upper back. Drop your head and look at your navel, tucking your tailbone under. Feel the stretch in the upper back. Repeat.

### WATCHPOINT
When practising the *cat stretch*, ensure that your hips are directly over your knees. Keep the arms straight, with wrists directly below the shoulders and the fingers spread. It is the upper body that is being worked here, not the weight-bearing joints of the lower body, so focus on moving the upper spine, neck and head and keep your hips fixed.

# Classical inspiration

 **Here we show an expert performing two modern classical poses taught in most yoga classes: swan stretch and dog stretch. This level of grace and flexibility is inspiring but all of us will benefit from our own practice of these positions.**

## INVERTED POSES

Wonderfully energizing, inverted poses are popular with yoga practitioners. The two best known poses – the headstand and the shoulderstand – are difficult to get into and dangerous to topple out of. A good alternative is the inverted *dog stretch*, where your head is held lower than your heart for a few minutes, but you are in a stable position. Begin with the swan stretch to elongate your spine and neck in preparation.

## BENEFICIAL CHANGE IS HEALING

Even if we cannot yet achieve the perfect *dog stretch*, we can nevertheless work on those three basic activities that bring about the beneficial changes in us that we call "healing": self-discipline, self-awareness and self-surrender. More than two thousand years ago, the great yoga master, Patanjali, called them the "practical steps on the path of yoga". They underlie all healing and achievement – not only in yoga but also in other

## SWAN STRETCH

▲ Sit on your heels with toes touching and spine straight. Bring your head to the floor (with your buttocks still touching your heels). Stretch your spine, taking your arms forward into the swan stretch.

aspects of our lives. Everything worthwhile requires enthusiastic practice, commitment and understanding of the principles involved. We need to let go of our negative conditioning, bad habits and poor self-image to move forward.

## WATCHPOINT

If you have heart or breathing problems avoid the inverted *dog stretch*. Experiment first with a *standing forward bend*. You can either hold the forward bend briefly or come up to standing with each breath IN.

## DOG STRETCH

**1** Begin in the *swan stretch*. Shift your weight forward on to hands and knees in the *cat stretch*. Tuck your toes under. Lift your buttocks into the air, keeping your knees bent. Stand on your toes, taking your weight forward into shoulders, arms and hands. In this position, work to open your chest and bring your shoulders closer to the floor.

**2** Finally, straighten your legs and bring your heels to the floor (if you can). Breathe deeply throughout, holding the position for as long as you can without strain. To come out of it, lower your knees to the floor and rest your heart in the *swan stretch* for a few moments before raising your head and trunk into an upright position, sitting on heels.

# Final relaxation

**Every yoga session should end with winding down, final relaxation and a "grounding" ritual. These practices may be the most important part of your yoga session, as they promote an attitude that brings healing at many levels.**

WINDING DOWN

End your yoga session with some final stretching and some deep breathing. These are very relaxing activities, highly recommended at any time, and especially before going to sleep at night. They "switch on" the branch of the autonomic nervous system that activates the body's essential maintenance and repairs necessary for healing. Feel that "all is well" – as it nearly always is in the Now. This is a deeply peaceful and healing attitude in itself. We can always feel that way, even when stuck in a traffic jam. Why get fearful and uptight about something that is not a physical threat? Usually it is because we are reacting according to our outdated mental patterns of thinking.

These patterns, these basic attitudes, can soon be changed by practising our "all is well" yoga techniques at every opportunity, many times each day – especially when feeling stressed.

▼ *SAVASANA* IS AN IDEAL POSITION FOR MENTAL AND PHYSICAL RELAXATION.

## Final relaxation

This is "winding down" practised in a position (such as *savasana*) where the body is totally supported so that all muscles can relax completely. This, in turn, reinforces the attitude that "all is well" – otherwise the large "fighting and fleeing" muscle groups in the arms and legs would be clenched, and probably the jaw too.

As you relax, take your mind on a journey around your body to discover whether any muscles have tightened up again. If so, breathe OUT slowly while sending a message of letting go into those places that are holding on to tension. Final relaxation is not

▲ If the small of your back arches away from the floor, support your head and bend your legs.

a time to fall asleep. Rather, keep an attentive mind in an inert body, watching out for the slightest tension in order to dissolve it.

## Grounding

After 5–15 minutes' deep relaxation, come out very slowly, maintaining the inner attitude of peace and trust (Love), while being ready for and aware of (Light) the challenges of Life. Become conscious of your body and surroundings before sitting up. Once sitting, you can touch the ground with your head (Light) and hands (Love) as you celebrate your Life.

# What is meditation?

**People have always had the need to seek inner peace and relaxation, for spiritual and health reasons and self-realization. By practising just 20 minutes a day, you can achieve and enjoy the wonderful benefits of meditation.**

Just what is meditation? Most simply put, it is sitting and relaxing. Many people find that their lives are so full of the demands of work, family, friends and organized leisure pursuits that they have no time to "stand and stare". Some are so caught up in planning and working towards the future that they take little pleasure from the here and now. In their bustle to "get on", they miss out on the simple pleasures of life: the changing seasons, birds singing or children discovering the beauty of life.

Beauty and joy, however, can be experienced in the most industrial of landscapes or the most difficult living situations. Meditation is a good way of taking time out and allowing yourself to tune into and appreciate the moment, whether you happen to be walking along the seashore, sitting by a stream, or just noticing and enjoying the intensity of silence in a still room.

▼ MEDITATION CAN HELP YOU TO REACH YOUR INNER RESPONSES TO THE WORLD AROUND YOU.

▲ Sit with your feet flat on the ground and your hands resting in your lap.

## Getting comfortable

Rather than push yourself to adopt some strained physical position for meditation, just relax – sit in a chair or stroll through your favourite landscape at a steady pace. It is better not to slump or lie down when you are learning to meditate, as this could lull you into sleep: a state of relaxed attentiveness is what is desired. If you sit on a chair, do so with your feet flat on the floor, hands resting in your lap or on the arms of the chair, and your head comfortably balanced. If you are walking, take slow, careful steps – be aware of the movement of each foot, and its contact with the ground beneath.

## Being here and now

Above all, meditation is about staying with the moment, about being in touch with your surroundings and your inner world. To experience this spirituality, you need not be a part of any organized religion. Although most religions do use some form of focused contemplation to promote spiritual awareness, meditation is also a technique that can be used for stress management or simply as a method to gain self-awareness.

Meditation is a pleasant way to gain deep relaxation, one in which you allow precious time for yourself. Simply meditating on a regular basis can be beneficial, but using words and images while practising can promote a marked improvement in your general well-being or in a specific area of life. It can even help you gain confidence when planning for upcoming events.

The benefits of meditation come from regular use. If under stress, you may find that meditating twice daily will restore composure and reduce irritability. It is best to allow at least ten, and ideally 20, minutes in meditation at each session.

# Gaining the meditative state

**The first rule in approaching the meditative state is to learn to relax completely. When you stop working, the tension that has built up in your mind and body remains, and this must be diffused before you can benefit from rest.**

A programme of exercises will loosen contracted muscles and make you feel refreshed, revitalized and physically relaxed. As well as unwinding the stresses in your body, exercise has the added benefit of releasing mental tension, so it can be a helpful prelude to every meditation session.

If strains and tensions are allowed to build up in the body, they may lead to a variety of aches and pains, as well as increasing mental strain and diminishing co-ordination and efficiency. A single session of exercises for relaxation will instantly refresh and calm you. Loosening your muscles will also make you aware of areas of tension in your body, so that you can give some attention to the causes: improving your posture and the way you sit at your desk, or changing the shoes you wear when you are constantly on your feet.

Relaxation reduces not only muscular tension, but also rates of respiration and digestion, blood pressure and heart rate. It also increases the efficiency of the internal organs and the immune system.

▶ RELAX IN A POSITION THAT IS COMFORTABLE FOR YOU.

While it is vital to relieve tension when you feel it building up into aching or stiffness, it is better to avoid such a build-up by incorporating relaxation exercises into your daily routine. Use them to stretch stiff muscles when you get up in the morning, or during a mid-morning or afternoon break from work. At bedtime, taking a few minutes to release tension in your neck, back and shoulders will aid sound, relaxing sleep. Training your body to relax fully will calm your mind and prepare it for the meditative state.

### STANDING RELAXATION EXERCISES FOR NECK, BACK AND SHOULDERS

**1** Stand upright with your arms stretched above your head. Rise up on your toes and stretch further still.

**2** Drop forward, keeping your knees relaxed, and let your arms, head and shoulders hang heavy and loose for a while.

**3** Shake your head and arms vigorously, then slowly return to a standing position. Repeat the exercise two or three times.

**2** Drop forward, allowing your head and arms to relax completely. Return to the starting position and repeat the exercise, staying aware of the changing tensions in the muscles.

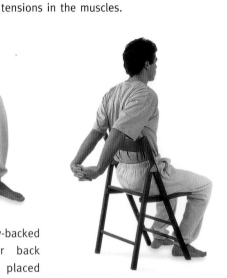

**1** Sit upright in a firm, low-backed chair with your lower back supported and feet placed squarely on the floor, hip-width apart. Raise your arms above your head and stretch them upwards, feeling the pull in your upper body. Look upwards and hold the stretch for 20–30 seconds.

**3** To stretch the back, link your hands together behind the chair, and lift your arms slightly. Lean back gradually, arching your back over the chair, hold for 10 seconds, then repeat.

# The three "S"s of meditation

**When you begin to meditate, there are three things that you can focus on to make the process easier and more fluid. These will help you to "close off" the outside world and concentrate on the rich vastness of the inner world.**

### STILLNESS

Being able to sit relaxed and completely still is very important: it will enable you to drift into the state of awareness where your inner world can be reached and enjoyed. If you start to fidget or become aware that you are not comfortable, the stream of concentration will be broken. The ideal is to maintain stillness throughout the meditation.

### SILENCE

Many people use personal stereos to try and block out the noise around them, but this can be very counterproductive: it is much better to meditate during a quiet time of day and learn to create inner silence. This will encourage your mind to see images and hear sounds coming from your inner self. The more you allow images and feelings to surface, the less you will be distracted. A teacher once said that when you can meditate on a busy railway platform, you will know you can really meditate.

▲ MEDITATION IS THE BEST GATEWAY TO INNER WISDOM; FIND TIME EVERY DAY TO INCREASE YOUR ABILITY.

### SENSITIVITY

When you begin any new meditation technique, it is important to listen, watch and perceive whatever images, symbols, sounds and other sensations appear in your mind. These may be vague and fleeting at first, but by noticing and focusing on them, you will aid the whole process. You will become more still and quiet, and your overall awareness will become sharper – in meditation and, eventually, in the rest of your life.

# Breathing and meditation

**The power of proper breathing should not be underestimated – it oxygenates the blood, aiding thought processes and boosting physical energy. It also assists the flow of toxins out of the bloodstream, thus reducing the effects of stress.**

▲ COUNT EACH BREATH FROM ONE TO TEN.

In meditation, your breath provides an ever-present and easily accessible focus on which to concentrate – you are always breathing. Many schools of meditation advocate using the breath in various ways, such as imagining that the breath originates at certain points in the body. The areas usually focused on are the "hara" just below the navel and the "tan tien", the heart in the centre of the chest. The crown of the head, the base of the spine and the soles of the feet may all be included in the awareness.

There are many ways of concentrating the mind in order to distract the inner "voice" that chatters incessantly, worrying and becoming obsessive about problems or people:

• Slowly count your breaths, from one to ten.

• Notice the physical changes at the nostrils and the abdomen, as your breath moves in and out.

• Notice the inner stillness as you change from exhalation to inhalation, from inhalation to exhalation.

• Conjure up an image that evokes a feeling of joy and serenity. This could be a beautiful natural scene with mountains or ocean waves, the sun's rays or a child. Breathe the image into your heart.

◀ IMAGINE EACH BREATH ORIGINATES AT THE HEART.

## CHAKRA-BALANCING MEDITATION

The following exercise is a powerful way of activating and balancing personal energies, thus improving your overall health and wellbeing.

**1** Sit comfortably, with your spine straight and relaxed. Breathe from your lower abdominal area and focus your attention on the first chakra, at the base of your spine. Imagine that you are breathing in and out of this point, and sense the external energies brought in by your breath.

**2** Bring your attention to your second chakra, above the genitals, and repeat the process.

**3** Continue the exercise through all the chakras, until you reach the crown chakra. You may find that with some of the chakras, the energies are a bit stagnant and a little extra time and attention is needed to bring them into focus.

**4** Now review each chakra in turn, from bottom to top, and imagine you are unblocking the natural energy flow in each and redressing the balance between them.

**5** Be aware that the base chakra connects you to the earth and the crown chakra to cosmic energies; sense the integration between your physical and spiritual energies with that of the whole universe.

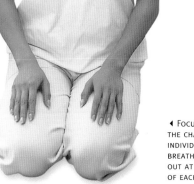

◀ FOCUS ON THE CHAKRAS INDIVIDUALLY AND BREATHE IN AND OUT AT THE POINT OF EACH ONE.

# Postures for meditation

**Meditation is a personal experience, but one that you need not practise in private. You can meditate almost anywhere – on the bus, in the park, or sitting at your desk – but it is important to find a position that feels comfortable for you.**

When choosing a position in which to meditate, remember that you should feel relaxed without drifting off to sleep. In addition, you should be able to remain still for the period of meditation without experiencing any numbness or cramp in your limbs, as this would be distracting and counterproductive. Experiment with the following suggestions until you discover which position feels best for you.

SITTING ON YOUR HEELS
This posture is a good one for your back, as it keeps the spine straight. Your feet should be relaxed, with the toes pointing backwards. Rest your hands lightly on your lap. Put a cushion underneath your feet if you wish.

SITTING ON THE FLOOR
Sit comfortably with your back straight and supported by a wall, with your legs outstretched and feet together. Rest your hands on your thighs.

SITTING ON A CHAIR
Choose a firm chair that provides good support for your lower back. Put your feet together, resting them flat on the floor. Rest your hands on your thighs. Keep your back straight but relax your shoulders, and keep your head erect.

## THE LOTUS POSITION

**1** The half-lotus is the simpler version: bend one leg so that the foot rests under the opposite inner thigh. Place the second foot on top of the thigh of the first leg. Keep the spine upright, and rest the hands lightly on the knees.

**2** To achieve the full lotus position, one leg should be bent with the foot resting on top of your other thigh; then bend your other leg so that the foot crosses over the first leg on to the opposite thigh.

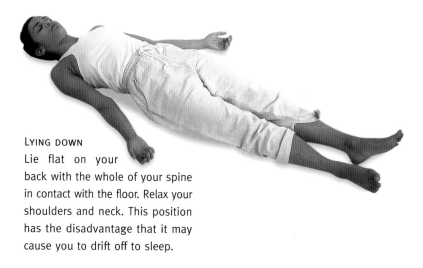

### LYING DOWN
Lie flat on your back with the whole of your spine in contact with the floor. Relax your shoulders and neck. This position has the disadvantage that it may cause you to drift off to sleep.

# Using sounds

Many adherents of transcendental meditation and religious groups talk of using a sound to assist with meditation. The repetition of a phrase, a word or a sound creates the alpha state by an almost hypnotic focus upon the sound.

An effortless sound, repeated with the natural rhythm of breathing, can have the same soothing, mentally liberating effect as the constant natural sound of running water, rustling leaves or a beating heart. The single sound, or mantra as it is known, is used to blot out the chatter of intrusive thoughts, allowing the mind to find repose.

Speaking or chanting a mantra as a stream of endless sound is a very ancient method of heightening an individual's awareness by concentrating the senses. The simple gentle sound "om" or "aum" is sometimes known as the first mantra, which is literally an instrument of thought. From the ancient Hindu language, the curving Sanskrit symbol for this primordial word represents the states of consciousness: waking, dreaming, deep dreamless sleep and the transcendental state.

The Hare Krishna movement is well known for its chant, which is repeated over and over again,

and can lead its members to become "high" – again the effects of endorphin release. However, the sound need not be a special word or incantation; something simple and meaningful will be just as effective. Any word that appeals to you will do, repeated with the outflow of breath – silently in the mind, or spoken out loud.

▲ THE CONSTANT, YET VARIABLE SOUND OF RUNNING WATER CAN BE ESPECIALLY SOOTHING AND THERAPEUTIC.

# Using touch

You can use your sense of touch in a soothing way to induce a state of meditation when you are under stress. Young children do this when they take a smooth ribbon or blanket end to hold and manipulate whenever they feel tense.

For centuries in the Middle East, people have benefited from the soothing sense of touch by using strings of worry beads: these are passed rhythmically

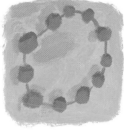

◀ FEEDING WORRY BEADS THROUGH YOUR FINGERS CAN HELP TO FOCUS AND CALM THE MIND.

through the fingers during times of stress and difficulty, in order to focus the mind and calm anxiety. The beads' uniform size, gentle round shapes, smooth surfaces and rhythmic, orderly clicking as they pass along their string all assist the state of mind.

You can use one or two smooth, rounded stones or crystals in the same way, passing them from one hand to the other, and concentrating on their temperature, shape and surface.

Alternatively, choose an object with a soothing and tactile quality that particularly appeals to you, such as a favourite velvet or silk scarf, which you can feed slowly from one hand to the other as you concentrate on clearing your mind.

▶ THE SMOOTH FEEL OF A SILK SCARF BETWEEN YOUR HANDS MAY HELP TO LULL YOU INTO THE MEDITATIVE STATE.

# Using colours

**Some colours are associated with relaxation. Summoning up and concentrating on these can be a helpful way to clear the mind of tension. They can be an ideal entry into the quiet of a meditation session.**

Sit with your eyes closed, and be aware of the first colour that comes into your mind: it may be any colour of the rainbow – though red and purple are common. Slowly let the colour change to blue or green, allowing it to fill the whole of your mind's eye and replace all other colours; pink hues are also beneficial. A feeling of relaxation will grow as the new colour builds in your mind. When it is complete, you will experience pleasant feelings of inner peace and stillness.

### Breathing in colour
You can help the colour to build by associating it with your breathing. Establish a comfortable rhythm of breathing, and focus on it until your mind is clear. Allow the colour to fill your mind's eye; then, as you breathe in, imagine the colour filling your body, from the soles of your feet right up to the top of your head.

### Colour visualization exercise
Shut your eyes and breathe calmly and regularly, focusing on your breathing. As you inhale, imagine that you are sitting on a soft lawn in a peaceful garden. Sense the cool freshness of the green surrounding you. As you exhale, imagine the silken magenta of a rose. Breathe in again and let the cleansing green fill your mind. Repeat this exercise once or twice, then sit quietly for a few moments.

▶ Try to become aware of the wonderful colours of the natural world, such as in this field of brightly coloured tulips.

## COLOUR PROPERTIES

Colours are associated with various qualities, so choose a colour to suit your current needs. Its complementary colour is shown in brackets. Often meditators visualize moving from their chosen colour to its complement – a way of creating change. Or they may move from one colour to another to gain these qualities.

- Red: vitality, energy, strength and will power (turquoise)
- Orange: happiness and laughter (blue)
- Yellow: intellect and objectivity (violet)
- Green: cleansing and harmony (magenta)
- Turquoise: strengthens the immune system, counteracts disease (red)
- Blue: peace and relaxation, restful sleep (orange)
- Violet: beauty, dignity, self-respect (yellow)
- Magenta: release of obsessional thoughts and memories (green)

# YOGA AND MEDITATION
# TREATMENTS

The pace of life is fast and demanding and it is easy to get lost in the outer world. More and more people are suffering from stress-related illnesses ranging from everyday tension headaches to depression and serious nervous disorders. Many of these health problems can be related to imbalances in the chakras (energy centres).

Beginning with more about chakra healing – and its relationship to life and love – this section encourages us to "come back" and explore our inner world using deep relaxation and meditation techniques. These have the power to heal old wounds, bringing clarity of vision and purpose. There are also specific exercises for cleansing and clearing the mind, improving stamina and focusing on goals.

# More about the chakras

**The chakras correspond to points along the physical spine and seem to co-ordinate the emotional qualities and basic attitudes that create our "inner" world and reflect out into our lives. Balancing the chakras balances our lives.**

We can change the state of our autonomic nervous system from the fright-fight-flight syndrome to "all is well" by working with the chakras. Use awareness, movement and stillness in those areas of the body that feel closed or weak and are in need of energy, healing and rebalancing.

▼ STRONG, EARTHBOUND POSTURES DRAW ENERGY TO THE LIFE CHAKRAS.

### THE THREE LIFE CHAKRAS
These correspond to points on the spine in the abdominal cavity:

**1** At the base of the spine. This chakra is concerned with physical safety/survival. Here we trust (positive) or fear (negative) the world. Yoga helps us to stand firm with strength and courage.

**2** At the sacrum. This chakra is concerned with sexual/social interaction. Here we enjoy (positive) or shrink from (negative) the company of others. Yoga helps us to have more fun and friendship in our lives.

**3** At the solar plexus. This chakra is concerned with self-confidence. Here we work to succeed (positive) or are obsessed with self-image (negative). Yoga helps us to live our lives with enthusiasm and commitment.

### THE TWO LOVE CHAKRAS
These correspond to points on the spine in the thoracic cavity:

**4** Situated behind the heart (and related to the arms and hands). This chakra is concerned with personal

▲ STRAIGHTEN YOUR SPINE AND OPEN YOUR CHEST TO BALANCE THE LOVE CHAKRAS.

These lie in the skull cavity:

**6** Situated behind the brow. This chakra is concerned with mental activity. We focus our thoughts clearly (positive) or live in a mental fog (negative). Yoga helps us to relax and be more aware that "all is well" beneath the noise of our mental chatter.

**7** Situated on the crown. This chakra is concerned with our attitudes and spiritual purpose. We grow in wisdom (positive) or stagnate in self-centredness (negative). Yoga helps us to relax and embrace ourselves and others.

▼ PRACTISE FORWARD BENDS TO SEND BLOOD TO THE LIGHT CHAKRAS.

relationships. Here we share with others (positive) or "keep ourselves to ourselves" (negative). Yoga helps us to accept both the joy and the vulnerability of relating.

**5** Situated behind the throat (and connected to speech and hearing). This chakra is concerned with creative communication. We express our thoughts and feelings while listening to those of others (positive) or we choose to "hide behind words" without hearing (negative). Yoga helps us to share our truth more honestly.

# Relaxing body and mind

**After relaxing body and mind we can unwind at those deeper levels where old fears, hurts and resentments lurk, sapping energy and joy. Once accessed, these "sore places" in our psyches can be healed.**

YOGA RELAXATION

Follow the instructions, moving systematically "inwards" and then "outwards" again. With practice you will know what you can do in ten minutes or in twenty. Allow time to "return" to the everyday world and to ground yourself thoroughly. Practise daily and this technique will bring deep and healing changes. You could tape the instructions to play while you relax.

**1** Remember your *sankalpa*.

**2** Settle your body in *savasana* – you can cover yourself with a blanket if needed. Have your spine and head totally supported and your shoulders and hips loose. Once settled, do not move.

**3** Settle your breathing.

**4** Take your mind to each part of the body in turn and connect with that part. Always use the same order: right thumb, each finger in turn, palm, wrist, forearm, elbow, upper arm, shoulder, right side of chest, of waist, right hip, front of thigh, back of thigh, front of knee, back of knee, calf, shin, ankle, heel, ball of foot, top of foot, big toe, each toe in turn. Repeat on left side. Go around twice if you have time. This practice connects our minds with our bodies and heals the body-mind split that can cause many problems.

**5** Move energy from the feet and up the spine – through the chakras – as you breathe IN and down as

▼ PLACING BLANKETS UNDER YOUR BACK HELPS TO OPEN UP YOUR CHEST.

▲ You may find *savasana* easier if you support your knees and head.

you breathe OUT, healing and restoring balance at all levels. Wash away all burdens on the tide of energy moving back down to the Earth through your feet.

**6** Visualize a place that means "spiritual home" to you – inside a sacred building, in a garden or by the sea, or in your own heart space where the Eternal Flame burns brightly. Settle yourself quietly and reverently in this space and feel its vibrations healing you.

**7** Silently repeat your *sankalpa* three times, with deep commitment and intent.

COMING OUT OF RELAXATION
When you are ready, start to come out of relaxation. Look at the place you are in and say goodbye to it, remembering that it is always there for you to return to. Begin to breathe consciously and deeply, revving up the "engines" of your body, ready for movement. Move your fingers and toes, your wrists and ankles. Stretch your limbs with a long, contented sigh, then a yawn, then a sigh again. Curl up, roll on to your side and sit up slowly when you are fully awake. Ground yourself thoroughly before getting up.

▼ Find your most comfortable position. Settle into it and relax.

# Yoga and common ailments

**Prolonged stress contributes to many health problems by overworking some systems and causing congestion or stagnation in others. Yoga rebalances the nervous system, removes toxic build-up from the body and is holistic.**

POLLUTION IN THE BODY

The immune system is programmed to remove (through activities such as pain, inflammation, fever, etc.) all foreign bodies that enter the body. These can be bacteria, viruses, food additives, poisons in food, water and air, recreational and medicinal drugs (the side-effects). We ingest so much that is unnatural nowadays that the body gets stressed and confused as to what is friend and what is foe and starts attacking itself.

▼ A HEALTHY DIET PLAYS AN IMPORTANT PART IN BOOSTING YOUR IMMUNE SYSTEM.

Many common conditions such as addiction, allergies, asthma, auto-immune diseases or chronic fatigue, are largely due to environmental stress.

The yogic answer to stress from pollution is two-fold. First, it works to reduce overall stress by rebalancing the autonomic nervous system so that the fright-fight-flight response is less easily triggered and the "all is well" response becomes the norm. Secondly, it tries to avoid ingesting pollutants through lifestyle and diet. This includes our diet of mental and emotional negativity as well as physical poisons. In the end, if we attend to the warning signals of distress, we create a happier and more fulfilling lifestyle.

ADDICTION

All yoga is very helpful. Relaxation with *sankalpa* and meditation brings release, healing and recovery when practised persistently with other (especially group) therapies.

### ALLERGIES

Regular yoga practice can reduce the need for medication. Consider your diet, as this is often how substances that are poisonous (to you) enter the system. Practise relaxation and meditation to reduce stress, as this can trigger allergic reactions.

### ARTHRITIS

Gentle exercise brings relief. If only some joints are affected, practise in the evening, having loosened up during the day. If inflammation is general the morning may be better. Avoid all exercise during a period of "flare up". Take great care with replacement joints and try to avoid positions that put pressure on weight-bearing joints. Choose sitting or lying positions for initial limbering and breathing and then do standing sequences slowly, with deep breathing and rests.

### ASTHMA

Do what feels comfortable, slowly and without strain. Use your breath as a monitor, breathing deeply through your nose. Stop to rest at the first signs of breathing

▲ DO YOU HAVE A FAVOURITE SPOT? RELAX AND SPEND TIME "JUST BEING".

discomfort. Relax propped up. Watch your diet to avoid constipation. Relaxation and meditation reduce the levels of stress that can trigger asthma attacks.

### AUTO-IMMUNE DISEASES AND CHRONIC FATIGUE

Keep active and cheerful through regular yoga practice, but avoid stress and fatigue by relaxing mind and body and working with *sankalpa* for serenity and a positive attitude.

### Back, neck and head pain

Pain and discomfort in these areas may be caused by poor posture, which can result from prolonged stress (feeling overwhelmed or defeated), lack of exercise and too much sitting.

### Improving posture

Realigning the spine, gently and persistently through regular yoga practice, can change both posture and attitudes. Practise relaxation and chakra meditation (propped up to be upright and comfortable) to strengthen the positive aspects of the chakras – especially those in the region of the pain. Reduce stress by practising *alternate nostril breathing* and deep relaxation in any comfortable position. Work on the muscles that hold the spine in place with *body-mind breathing*

and gentle isometric "muscle squeezing" to improve spinal posture and to reduce injury and the body's need to protect itself by going into spasm.

### Lower back pain

Lie on the floor with knees bent to take all pressure off the spine. Move the spine gently to ease discomfort. The upturned beetle is also helpful: move the knees gently in all directions to ease the lower back. Move the head from side to side and loosen the shoulders for the upper back and neck. Keep the chin tucked in.

### Headache

Pressure in the cervical or thoracic spine through habitually jutting the chin forward and/or slouching creates "traffic congestion" and is

▾ BACK PAIN CAN BE RELIEVED BY GENTLY MASSAGING YOUR SPINE AGAINST THE FLOOR.

a common cause of headaches. Loosen the neck muscles with the head upside down in a forward bend, standing, sitting on a chair or lying prone over the edge of a bed. Take short yogic breaks between daily activities, especially those involving the eyes.

## CARDIOVASCULAR/RESPIRATORY PROBLEMS

These conditions can result from prolonged stress, when the nervous system's fright-fight-flight response is switched on more or less permanently, ready for "action" and "excitement". Eventually the overused systems falter, while the underused systems are unable

▲ INVERTED POSTURES CAN HELP A HEADACHE, BUT BE WARY IF YOU HAVE CARDIOVASCULAR OR RESPIRATORY PROBLEMS.

to provide essential nourishment, repair and recuperation. When the "all is well" response is blocked through prolonged stress we probably feel angry and exhausted. The yogic answer is to change our whole outlook upon life, to slow down yet keep as active as possible, and to learn to enjoy simple pleasures and a peaceful life.

Yoga exercise is helpful. Use your breath as a monitor, stopping if the breathing speeds up. Deep slow breathing, focusing on the OUT breath, induces a slow pulse rate and reduces stress. Avoid head-below-heart and arms-above-head positions if they make you feel breathless or dizzy. Relax and meditate regularly.

▼ TO CALM THE MIND, TRY THIS SIMPLE MEDITATION. LOOK AT A CANDLE FLAME, THEN CLOSE YOUR EYES, KEEPING THE IMAGE IN YOUR "MIND'S EYE" AS LONG AS YOU CAN.

### Depression

The term depression is often loosely used to describe anything from "feeling the blues" for a day or two to a prolonged and severe condition that requires medical treatment and supervision.

Yoga can alleviate this painful mental and emotional stress by rebalancing the Life, Light and Love energies. Focus on activating the Life chakras to increase vitality. Go for brisk walks and practise strong, invigorating standing postures to get the energy flowing. Depression can create deep fatigue, so exercise in short bursts with rests between each sequence – but do keep at it. Start and end your sessions with *alternate nostril breathing*. Avoid meditation and do not practise deep relaxation for longer than ten minutes, focusing on a positive *sankalpa*. Keep a spiritual diary to record and release distress. Re-read it periodically and notice how much yoga is lifting your spirits.

### Digestive and other problems

The fright-fight-flight response, while revving up (and eventually exhausting) some systems, denies

▼ Be positive and value yourself – you are always your own best friend.

▲ Writing things down eases the burden on the mind and reduces anxiety.

Breathe deeply and relax often to reduce stress. Use *sankalpa* and meditate on the chakras and how both their positive and negative qualities promote or block the "all is well" response that creates healing and a balanced lifestyle.

▼ Standing postures can invigorate and lift your spirits.

energy to all non-essential functions at the same time. If this response becomes your habitual pattern, many of the body's systems (such as the digestive, eliminatory and hormonal systems) become depleted and will then malfunction or become diseased.

Yoga helps to rebalance the nervous system and reduce anxiety (and therefore the production of adrenalin). Avoid lying prone, or putting pressure on the abdomen in postures. Improve spinal alignment with deep breathing. Practise yoga before eating.

# Cleansing the mind

**Meditating lets you focus on yourself with greater clarity. It allows you to sift through all your scattered energies, and release thoughts and desires you no longer need. Try this exercise to cleanse your psyche with healing rays of colour.**

**1** Close your eyes and imagine that you are sitting in a green meadow. A cool, crystal-clear stream runs nearby, with abundant fragrant flowers all around. It is a fine, bright day with a gentle breeze; the sky is blue, with a scattering of soft, white clouds.

**2** Choose a colour that you need (see pages 158–61) for your personal healing and well-being.

**3** Choose one of the clouds above you and fill it with the colour until it starts to shimmer with its sparkling light.

**4** Let the cloud float over you. Allow it to release a coloured shower that envelops you with a sweet, sparkling mist, like stars cascading in all directions.

**5** The mist settles on your skin and is gently absorbed, until it has completely saturated your system with its healing vibration.

**6** Allow the hue to run through your bloodstream for 3–4 minutes,

giving your body a therapeutic colour wash.

**7** Let the pores of your skin open so that the coloured vapour can escape, taking any toxins with it. When the vapour runs clear, close your pores again.

**8** Sit quietly with your cleared, healed body and mind for a few minutes. Take three deep breaths, releasing each gently, then open your eyes.

▸ MEDITATE OUT OF DOORS TO CONNECT TO YOUR HIGHER SPIRITUAL DIMENSION.

# Maintaining stamina

In this meditation, you will use the enlivening colour gold to recharge your body and mind, letting its warmth restore your physical energy and lift your spirits. It is perfect for use in the midst of an active period, to help restore or maintain stamina.

**1** Recline in a comfortable position and take a deep breath in. When you inhale, imagine yourself lying on a floating sunbed on the ocean or in a swimming pool, gently moving with the waves of the water.

**2** Look up at the sky – it is pale blue, with an arch of pure gold, high up. Focus on this shimmering band of sun-gold.

**3** After a few moments, allow the arch to vibrate gently, so that cascades of its sparkling golden crystals float gently towards you.

**4** As they lightly touch your body, the crystals turn to golden dew drops that are absorbed into your skin.

**5** Feel the internal warmth deep within you, as the golden hue surges through you, warming your body and soul and creating a wonderful glow.

**6** Take a deep breath and, as you exhale, slowly open your eyes. Feel the way in which your mind and body have been recharged and revitalized.

# Personal development

**Affirmations are a deceptively simple device that can be used by anyone, and they prove remarkably effective. Try using this method while in the meditative state, having previously planned and memorized the affirmations involved.**

In using affirmations with meditation, you combine ease of communication with all parts of the mind and the effectiveness of repeated powerful phrases. The technique requires you to say to yourself, out loud, a positive statement about yourself as you wish to be. In order to make your affirmations effective, they should:

• be made in the present tense

• be positively phrased

• have an emotional reward.

If you notice what happens if you are asked not to think of elephants, you will realize why negatives (the words "no", "not", "never" and so on) have the opposite effect to that intended. Yours is the most influential voice in your life, because you believe it! Be aware of any negative statements that you make regularly about yourself, either to others or to yourself – "I am shy", "I am lacking in confidence", "I cannot", "I get easily nervous when . . ." and so on. These are all self-limiting beliefs that you will reinforce each time they slip into your conversation or mind. Now you will be able to use affirmations whenever you are meditating in order to change those beliefs: "I am strong", "I am able to do this", "I feel really confident when . . . "

▲ AFFIRMATIONS CHANGE THE WAY YOU THINK ABOUT YOURSELF AND THE WAY YOU ACT AND REACT.

# Peak performance

Visualization requires you to imagine yourself behaving, reacting and looking as you would wish to do in a given situation. This could be at an interview or a social gathering – any situation where peak performance is important to you.

In the same way that you can utilize your voice, so you can use your imagination. The imagination can stimulate emotions and can instil new attitudes in the mind. It can be a direct communication with your unconscious mind, and it can provide a powerful influence for improvements in your attitudes, behaviour patterns and overall confidence.

Imagine yourself at an important event. What will it mean for you? What will your reactions and those of people around you be? Most importantly, feel all the good feelings that will occur.

Imagination is like playing a video of the event in the mind's eye, from the beginning of the situation through to the perfect outcome. Get in touch with the feelings that will be there when you reach that outcome. Should any doubts or negative images creep into your "video", push them away and replace them with positive ones. Keep the scenario realistic, and base it upon real information from your past. Once you are happy with the images you are seeing, note the way you are standing and presenting yourself. Then allow yourself to view the scene from inside your imagined self. Now you can get in touch with the feelings and attitudes that will make the event successful. The best time to do this is when you are relaxed mentally and physically – during meditation. Teach yourself to expect new, positive outcomes. This can be combined with affirmations, to make the exercise doubly effective.

▶ REHEARSE THE FORTHCOMING EVENT IN YOUR MIND'S EYE SO THAT YOU ARE FULLY PREPARED.

# Aiding concentration

**The pressures that are experienced when studying for an exam or learning a new skill can disrupt concentration, and so one's ability to absorb information. A visual image used during meditation can help re-energize your ability to learn.**

• I enjoy moments of insight and understanding.

• I enjoy using my mind and expanding the boundaries of my knowledge.

• My memory forms links between the known and the new information.

• My learning ability improves with use.

• I concentrate so completely that nothing but an emergency can distract me.

Imagine a huge jigsaw puzzle spread out in front of you: it is a giant picture made up of many smaller images, and each image is a jigsaw puzzle in itself. Some images are nearly complete, others are only just starting to form, some even seem a confused jumble of unattached pieces. Focus your attention on one image, one part of the giant puzzle that is nearly complete but is still a little confusing.

A new piece comes into your hand and it fills a gap as it interlocks with all the surrounding pieces . . . The image suddenly becomes clear, and you can see it now. You have a wonderful feeling of achievement: that which was confusing is now fully understood. You feel as you do when a new piece of information interlocks with others and you understand the whole subject. This insight . . . the joy of understanding . . . is what makes learning so worthwhile.

Should you ever need to retrieve that piece of the puzzle, to answer a question of some kind, you know that all the interlocking pieces will arrive with it to give insight and understanding – you can select and use them as you wish. The memory is like a giant puzzle, and the moments of achievement when understanding and enlightenment occur are the joy of learning itself and an important part of life's beauty.

As you learn, so you enjoy total concentration as you study and gain information. Only an emergency could distract you. Learning is a continuous part of being alive.

# Achieving goals

**In all areas of life – personal relationships, social interactions and career – having a goal is important in focusing your attention and inner resources. A goal provides a sense of direction, and ultimately brings the joy of achievement.**

Be aware of the different areas of your life: work, social, emotional and spiritual. Select one for this exercise . . . think about what you want to achieve and describe your goal on paper before beginning.

While in the meditative state, imagine that you have achieved this goal. Surround yourself with the things or people that indicate that you have achieved the goal. Be as specific as you can . . . be aware of all you see, hear, touch or sense . . . Be there . . . make it real . . . be specific about colours . . . temperatures . . . lighting. Be there and know how it feels to have achieved that goal . . . how it affects your mood.

Now, from where you are at that moment of achieving that goal . . . look back . . . as though along a pathway of time . . . to where you were . . . and notice the stages of change . . . of movement towards achieving the goal . . . the actions

you have taken . . . the contacts that you have made . . . the people involved. Be aware of the smallest moments of change that have occurred, from the start of the journey to its fulfilment . . . Remain in touch with the feelings that will make it all worthwhile . . . feel more determined to take one step at a time . . . make just one change at a time . . . Become more determined to be successful in the achievement of your goal . . . Take the first step towards it, today.

▶ VISUALIZE YOURSELF TAKING ONE STEP AT A TIME TOWARDS YOUR GOAL.

# Index